Testing, Teaching, and Learning

A Guide for States and School Districts

Committee on Title I Testing and Assessment

Richard F. Elmore and Robert Rothman, Editors

Board on Testing and Assessment

Commission on Behavioral and Social Sciences and Education

National Research Council

NATIONAL ACADEMY PRESS
Washington, D.C.

NATIONAL ACADEMY PRESS • 2101 Constitution Avenue, N.W. • Washington, DC 20418

NOTICE: The project that is the subject of this report was approved by the Governing Board of the National Research Council, whose members are drawn from the councils of the National Academy of Sciences, the National Academy of Engineering, and the Institute of Medicine. The members of the committee responsible for the report were chosen for their special competences and with regard for appropriate balance.

The study was supported by The Pew Charitable Trusts (award 96000217-000), The Spencer Foundation (award 199700156), The William T. Grant Foundation (award 97179797), and the U.S. Department of Education (award R305U960001). Any opinions, findings, conclusions, or recommendations expressed in this publication are those of the author(s) and do not necessarily reflect the view of the organizations or agencies that provided support for this project.

International Standard Book Number 0-309-06534-8

Suggested citation: National Research Council (1999). *Testing, Teaching, and Learning: A Guide for States and School Districts.* Committee on Title I Testing and Assessment, Richard F. Elmore and Robert Rothman, editors. Board on Testing and Assessment, Commission on Behavioral and Social Sciences and Education. Washington, DC: National Academy Press.

Additional copies of this report are available from National Academy Press, 2101 Constitution Avenue, N.W., Washington, DC 20418.

Call (800) 624-6242 or (202) 334-3313 (in the Washington metropolitan area).

This report is also available online at http://www.nap.edu

Printed in the United States of America

Preface

Standards, assessment, and accountability have become a common concern of public policy toward education at the federal, state, and local levels. The reasons for this concern are deeply embedded in the politics and economics of the education sector over the past two decades—rising public expenditures, increasing centralization and equalization of education funding, and increasing concern among policy makers at all levels of government for the health and competitiveness of the American economy. Whatever one's position on the specifics, there is no avoiding the imperative for clearer definitions of the outcomes of schooling and clearer accounting for results.

In the midst of this debate, in 1994, the Congress reauthorized Title I, the largest single federal program for elementary and secondary education in the United States. The congressional debate around reauthorization of Title I was, in many ways, a reflection of the larger public debate that had been occurring around that time in thousands of local school boards, dozens of state legislatures, and many national commissions. In particular, the debate focused on the terms and conditions under which state agencies, local school districts, and schools would be accountable for the academic learning of disadvantaged students, who were the intended beneficiaries of Title I's supplemental funding. The 1994 amendments substantially shifted the focus of Title I, away from treating Title I recipients as a separate class of beneficiaries with their own particular needs and toward an emphasis on bringing educationally disadvantaged students into the academic mainstream, judging their academic success in the same terms as those of all other students. The 1994 amendments also brought Title I into alignment with the growing movement toward standards-based reform at the state and local levels, which focuses on setting high and clear goals for student academic learning and judging schools on the basis of their contributions to students' progress toward those goals.

In spring 1995, just before the reauthorization of Title I was set to take effect, the Board on Testing and Assessment of the National Research Council convened a workshop on the implications of Title I's new testing and assessment requirements for states and localities. This workshop, involving participants from federal, state, and local education agencies, as well as representatives of the research and testing community, surfaced a number of difficult technical and practical issues related to the implementation of the new requirements. As an outgrowth of this discussion, and with support from the U.S. Department of Education, the Pew Charitable Trusts, the Spencer Foundation, and the W.T. Grant Foundation, the National Research Council formed the Committee on Title I Testing and Assessment to look into these issues in greater depth. The committee began its work in November 1997.

The Committee on Title I Testing and Assessment was chartered for an explicitly practical purpose: to provide policy guidance to states and localities in using testing and assessment to improve the academic learning of students who are the intended beneficiaries of Title I. The committee was charged to assess research bearing on the use of testing and assessment for accountability purposes, to examine the experience of states and localities in this domain, and to develop a "decision framework that incorporates technical quality, effects on teaching and learning, costs and benefits, fairness and other criteria for evaluating assessment strategies." Hence, the committee's primary concern has been to provide practical guidance to states and localities in the design and implementation of standards-based assessments and accountability mechanisms, consistent with both state and local policy and with the requirements of Title I.

Reflecting its orientation toward practical guidance, the committee's membership represents a cross-section of expertise on testing and assessment issues, from state and local practitioners to academic researchers, and the full range of practical and conceptual concerns related to Title I assessment.

As the committee's work progressed, we came to a common understanding of the daunting task confronting states and localities in their attempts to create new forms of standards-based improvement and accountability in Title I. We agreed, for example, to focus on broad policy guidance to states and localities, organized around specific problems that any standards, assessment, and accountability system would have to solve, allowing for substantial variation and creativity in crafting specific solutions appropriate to specific state and local contexts. So this report focuses on "mid-range" advice, specific enough to provide useful guidance for policy makers and practitioners, broad enough to accommodate a wide range of solutions adapted to specific contexts. We also broadened the initial charge slightly to include discussion of issues of instruction and professional development for teachers and administrators in addition to issues of assessment and accountability. It became clear to us, as we explored the practical implications of Title I assessment and accountability, that the construction of assessment and accountability systems cannot be isolated from their purposes, which are to improve the quality of instruction and ultimately the learning of students. So we were inevitably drawn into the relationship between assessment and accountability issues and issues of large-scale improvement in teaching and learning.

In the five years or so since the reauthorization of Title I, progress on the assessment and accountability requirements of the law have been highly uneven. The 1994 law envisioned that by the year 2000 all states would have put in place content and performance standards, aligned with assessments of student performance, and coupled with systems for holding schools accountable for student learning. As the year 2000 and the next reauthorization of Title I approach, it is now clear that many states and localities are still struggling to meet the basic requirements of the law; some states and localities are meeting the requirements but having difficulties connecting assessments to a broad-scale strategy of instructional improvement; and some states have met the requirements of the law but discovered a new generation of problems related to the maintenance and improvement of their assessment and accountability systems.

The ambitious goals of the 1994 law are, in other words, still a work in progress in the field. This report is designed, to the extent possible, to speak to the entire range of states and districts, from the least to the most advanced. We also speak from the perspective that the struggle for increased focus and accountability in public education is a long-term project that will extend well beyond the present debate. We think our advice will be durable over the longer term, as public debate continues.

Because the implementation of Title I assessment is still a work in progress, the research available to the committee was limited. We have drawn on a broad body of research on testing and assessment issues generally, as well as the reports of previous NRC committees on specific questions of test development and utilization. But the practical nature of our charge and the limits of the evidence available to us have meant that we have also had to draw on the practical experience of committee members and outside experts in crafting our advice. Hence, this report relies heavily on expert advice from the field, in addition to scientific research.

Our hope is that state and local practitioners and policy makers will use this report as a guide to their continuing decisions in the development and improvement of new systems of assessment and accountability in Title I. It is *not* a simple template that prescribes a single approach or a single set of solutions. It is a framework, designed to lay out the major problems involved in the design of assessment and accountability systems, the knowledge that research and experience bring to bear on these problems, and the range of possible solutions to the problems. The framework also assumes that the purpose of assessment and accountability systems is to improve the quality of instruction in schools and school systems, rather than simply to measure and report school effectiveness.

Richard F. Elmore, *Chair*
Committee on Title I Testing and Assessment

The National Academy of Sciences is a private, nonprofit, self-perpetuating society of distinguished scholars engaged in scientific and engineering research, dedicated to the furtherance of science and technology and to their use for the general welfare. Upon the authority of the charter granted to it by the Congress in 1863, the Academy has a mandate that requires it to advise the federal government on scientific and technical matters. Dr. Bruce M. Alberts is president of the National Academy of Sciences.

The National Academy of Engineering was established in 1964, under the charter of the National Academy of Sciences, as a parallel organization of outstanding engineers. It is autonomous in its administration and in the selection of its members, sharing with the National Academy of Sciences the responsibility for advising the federal government. The National Academy of Engineering also sponsors engineering programs aimed at meeting national needs, encourages education and research, and recognizes the superior achievements of engineers. Dr. William A. Wulf is president of the National Academy of Engineering.

The Institute of Medicine was established in 1970 by the National Academy of Sciences to secure the services of eminent members of appropriate professions in the examination of policy matters pertaining to the health of the public. The Institute acts under the responsibility given to the National Academy of Sciences by its congressional charter to be an adviser to the federal government and, upon its own initiative, to identify issues of medical care, research, and education. Dr. Kenneth I. Shine is president of the Institute of Medicine.

The National Research Council was organized by the National Academy of Sciences in 1916 to associate the broad community of science and technology with the Academy's purposes of furthering knowledge and advising the federal government. Functioning in accordance with general policies determined by the Academy, the Council has become the principal operating agency of both the National Academy of Sciences and the National Academy of Engineering in providing services to the government, the public, and the scientific and engineering communities. The Council is administered jointly by both Academies and the Institute of Medicine. Dr. Bruce M. Alberts and Dr. William A. Wulf are chairman and vice chairman, respectively, of the National Research Council.

Acknowledgments

For all the reasons stated in the preface, this report could not have happened without support from a number of people, and the committee is grateful for their contributions. We want first of all to acknowledge our sponsors, who made the project possible and kept it going. At the U.S. Department of Education, Valena Plisko, Margaret McNeely, and Collette Roney showed a continuing interest in the project and kept us apprised of events and publications that would assist us in our work.

At the Pew Charitable Trusts, Robert B. Schwartz and C. Kent McGuire were instrumental in helping get the project off the ground. Their successor as education program officer, Edward F. Reidy, Jr., not only continued to support the project but also, during one meeting, donned his old Kentucky associate commissioner hat and helped the committee think through some of the nettlesome design issues involved in assessment and accountability at the state level. Sadly, Ed passed away shortly before this book went to press. We will miss his wisdom and his commitment to education reform.

At the Spencer Foundation, Mark Rigdon was an enthusiastic supporter of the work. At the William T. Grant Foundation, the former president, Beatrix Hamburg, helped nurture the project, and her successor, Karen Hein, maintained the support.

The committee was also aided greatly by individuals who participated in our meetings and helped us understand the complex issues involved in designing and implementing standards-based systems. Mary Jean LeTendre, director of compensatory education programs at the U.S. Department of Education, and Edward D. Roeber, then the director of the state education assessment center at the Council of Chief State School Officers, provided us with an overview of the state of play in Title I at the federal and state levels, respectively.

At our second meeting, a panel of educators from the school, district, and state levels described for us how tests were used at their sites. These were: Peter Behuniak of the Connecticut State Department of Education, Susanne Murphy of the Norwich (CT) Public Schools, Gloria Woods and Mary Russo of the Boston Public Schools, Mitchell Chester of the School District of Philadelphia, and Brenda Steele of Community District 2 in New York City. Three testing programs also lent us materials to review: Harcourt Brace Educational Measurement, New Standards, and the Connecticut State Department of Education.

At our third meeting, the committee heard from a panel of researchers and practitioners on the design issues involved in establishing assessments and accountability mechanisms. These were: Joan L. Herman of the National Center for Research on Evaluation, Standards, and Student Testing at the University of California, Los Angeles; James P. Spillane of Northwestern University; Edward Chittenden of the Educational Testing Service, Edward Reidy of the Pew Charitable Trusts (and formerly of Kentucky), and Lynn Winters of the Long Beach (CA) Unified School District.

The committee also commissioned several papers to address some critical areas in the research literature. Karen K. Wixson of the University of Michigan conducted an analysis of the alignment between standards and assessment in elementary reading in four states. J. Douglas Willms of the University of New Brunswick provided a helpful review of data analysis and reporting issues. M. Elizabeth Graue of the University of Wisconsin-Madison conducted an extensive literature review of assessment issues, focusing on early childhood assessments. Mark D. Reckase of Michigan State University reviewed the measurement issues associated with the Title I statute.

The Board on Testing and Assessment, the division within the National Research Council that launched the study, also provided considerable support to the committee as it conducted its work. William Taylor, a member of the board, attended nearly all the committee's meetings and lent us his substantial knowledge about Title I and the implementation of standards-based reform. Robert L. Linn, the board's chair, and Carl Kaestle, the vice chair, were very helpful and supportive.

Within the National Research Council, a number of individuals supported the project and helped us keep it moving forward. Barbara Boyle Torrey, the executive director of the Commission on Behavioral and Social Sciences and Education, and Alexandra Wigdor, the director of the Division on Education, Labor, and Human Performance, enthusiastically backed the project and lent wisdom and advice at key stages. Michael J. Feuer, the director of the Board on Testing and Assessment, was the guiding force behind the project and provided substantive advice and moral support all the way through. Patricia Morison helped guide us through the end game of report completion, review, and publication. Viola Horek helped us manage the complex finances of the project and provided support in innumerable ways. Christine McShane's skillful editing kept our tenses straight and our metaphors from mixing.

Dorothy Majewski, the senior project assistant, handled the logistics of our work with incredible dexterity and even more incredible good humor. Her ability to plan and manage complex arrangements and respond to last-minute requests and changes made our work much easier and much more enjoyable.

This report has been reviewed in draft form by individuals chosen for their diverse perspectives and technical expertise, in accordance with procedures approved by the NRC's Report Review Committee. The purpose of this independent review is to provide candid and critical comments that will assist the institution in making the published report as sound as possible and to ensure that the report meets institutional standards for objectivity, evidence, and responsiveness to the study charge. The review comments and draft manuscript remain confidential to protect the integrity of the deliberative process.

We wish to thank the following individuals for their participation in the review of this report: Stephen B. Dunbar, Iowa Testing Programs, University of Iowa; William Firestone, Graduate School of Education, Rutgers University; John F. Jennings, Center on Education Policy, Washington, D.C.; Margaret J. McLaughlin, Institute for the Study of Exceptional Children and Youth, University of Maryland; Daniel J. Reschly, Peabody College, Vanderbilt University; Alan Sheinker, Wyoming Department of Education, Cheyenne; and Richard Wagner, Department of Psychology, Florida State University. Although these individuals provided many constructive comments and suggestions, responsibility for the final content of this report rests solely with the authoring committee and the institution.

Richard F. Elmore, *Chair*
Robert Rothman, *Study Director*
Committee on Title I Testing and Assessment

Contents

Testing, Teaching, and Learning

Executive Summary

Title I of the Elementary and Secondary Education Act is the largest federal effort in precollegiate education. Created in 1965, when the federal government for the first time agreed to provide aid to elementary and secondary schools, the program was designed to level the playing field for disadvantaged students by providing financial assistance to their schools to compensate for the advantages enjoyed at schools with students from more affluent families. Now with an annual budget of approximately $8 billion—a fourth of the U.S. Department of Education's total annual budget—the program reaches more than 11 million students in two-thirds of all elementary schools and a fourth of all secondary schools.

The 1994 reauthorization of Title I represented a profound shift in the program; perhaps the most far-reaching changes were in the assessment arena. Specifically, the law requires states to develop challenging standards for student performance and assessments that measure student performance against the standards. Significantly, the law states that the standards and assessments are expected to be the same for all students, regardless of whether they are eligible for Title I. Thus for the first time, the 1994 statute enshrines into law the principle that Title I students are to be held to the same standards as all other students.

The record of states in implementing the new law shows that the 1994 statute poses a substantial challenge. For example, although nearly every state has adopted content standards, as the law requires, reviews of such standards show that their rigor and usefulness vary widely. In addition, only 21 states adopted performance standards by the law's deadline of 1997-1998; the rest received waivers to allow them more time. The uneven pace of implementation has led some commentators to suggest revising the program substantially.

The purpose of this document is to help states and districts meet the challenges posed by the law by guiding them in making appropriate decisions in implementing it. The Committee on Title I Testing and Assessment was charged with assessing research on the use of testing and assessment for accountability purposes, examining the experience of states and districts in this domain, and developing a "decision framework that incorporates technical quality, effects on teaching and learning, costs and benefits, fairness, and other criteria for evaluating assessment strategies." Our goal was to produce a practical guide for states and districts to use in developing the systems they were creating under the Title I law.

As we studied the research, examined our own experiences, and listened to testimony from state, district, and school officials, the committee kept in mind three underlying principles. First, the committee agreed that the purpose of assessments and accountability is to contribute to and support high levels of student learning, particularly for disadvantaged students who have lagged behind their more advantaged peers. Second, the committee agreed that the education improvement system should be conceived of and implemented as just that—a *system*. That is, the system should consist of a number of components, at various levels (classroom, school, school district, and state), each of which plays a role in measuring and contributing to student learning, yet which are interrelated, not separate from one another. Third, the committee agreed that a hallmark of the state and district systems should be continuous improvement, at all levels—for students, for teachers and administrators, and for the system itself. For these and other reasons, the committee developed criteria not for the one best system— which does not exist—but for systems that continually change and adapt to new knowledge and circumstances. States and districts need to continually monitor the effects of their policies and practices to ensure that they are attaining their goals. The committee's framework is appropriate for states and districts just starting out on redesigning their education improvement system, as well as for states and districts that have had redesigned systems in place for several years.

STANDARDS-BASED REFORM

The provisions of the 1994 law carry with them an implied "theory of action" that suggests how implementing them will achieve the larger goal of improving student learning.

As we understand it, the theory of action underlying the 1994 law is relatively straightforward. The centerpiece of the system is a set of challenging standards for student performance. By setting these standards for all students, states would hold high expectations for performance; these expectations would be the same regardless of students' backgrounds or where they attended school. Aligning assessments to the standards would allow students, parents, and teachers to monitor student performance against the standards. Providing flexibility to schools would permit them to make the instructional and structural changes needed for their students to reach the standards. And holding schools accountable for meeting the standards would create incentives to redesign instruction toward the standards and provide appropriate assistance to schools that need extra help.

Embedded in this theory are a number of assumptions that experience since 1994 has led the committee to call into question. Chief among these assumptions is the idea that teachers would institute effective practices if they had both the freedom and the motivation to do so. In addition, we question the assumption that motivated teachers would seek guidance about improving instruction and districts would provide the support teachers need, largely by making more widely available the existing array of professional development opportunities.

As a result of our examination of the theory of action, the committee concludes that the theory needs to be expanded to make explicit the link between standards, assessments, accountability, *instruction*, and learning. In our view, standards-based policies can affect student learning only if they are tied directly to efforts to build the capacity of teachers and administrators to improve instruction.

AN EXPANDED THEORY

What would such a system look like? In our view, the focus would be on *teaching and learning*, and the theory of action revolves around the links between all the elements and instruction. We call the expanded system an "education improvement system."

The theory of action behind an education improvement system relies on information and responsibility. Everyone in the system—students, parents, teachers, administrators, and policy makers at every level—needs high-quality information about the quality of instruction and student performance. At the same time, everyone needs to be responsible for fulfilling his or her role in improving results. The key is transparency: everyone should know what it is expected, what they will be measured on, and what the results imply for what they should do next.

Such a system is never "complete"; educators and policy makers continue to modify and adapt it as they learn from their own experience and the experience of others. States and districts need to examine each component, and the system as a whole, continually, to determine the extent to which it is achieving the goal of improving teaching and learning. In the following section we outline the criteria for the components.

COMPONENTS OF AN EDUCATION IMPROVEMENT SYSTEM

Standards

Standards for student performance are at the heart of the system. Standards set the expectations for student learning, and signal that all students, regardless of background or where they happen to attend school, are expected to demonstrate high levels of knowledge and skill. In addition, they focus the attention of everyone in the system on the results schooling is expected to achieve—academic performance—rather than the resources or effort put into the system.

Content standards spell out what students should know and be able to do in core subjects. They should be clear, parsimonious, and rigorous. Performance standards indicate the level of performance students should demonstrate. They should include: performance categories, performance descriptors, exemplars of performance in each category, and decision rules that enable educators to determine whether students have reached each category.

Assessments

Assessments in standards-based systems serve a number of purposes: guiding instruction, monitoring school and district performance, holding schools accountable for meeting performance goals, and more. No single instrument can serve all purposes well. Assessment should involve a range of strategies appropriate for inferences relevant to individual students, classrooms, schools, districts, and states.

In order to provide information on the quality of instruction and provide cues to help educators improve teaching and classroom practices, the overwhelming majority of standards-based assessments should be sensitive to effective instruction; that is, they should detect the effects of high-quality teaching. Districts, schools, and teachers should use the results of these assessments to revise their practices to help students improve performance.

Assessments are essential to measure the performance of all children. Yet, although 49 percent of children served by Title I are in grades 3 and below, the 1994 statute does not require states to establish assessments before grade 3. Without some form of assessment, schools and districts would have no way of determining the progress of this large group of students to ensure that they do not fall too far behind.

To measure the performance of young children, teachers should monitor the progress of individual children in grades K to 3 at multiple points in time by using direct assessments, portfolios, checklists, and other work sampling devices. And schools should be accountable for promoting high levels of reading and mathematics performance for primary grade students. For school accountability in grades 1 and 2, states and districts should gauge school quality through the use of sampling, rather than the assessment of every pupil.

Including students with disabilities and English-language learners in assessments also poses significant challenges. Although state policies vary widely, many states exclude large numbers of students with disabilities and English-language learners from assessment mandates. Others include such students but use measures that may not be appropriate.

States and districts should develop clear guidelines for accommodations that permit students with disabilities to participate in assessments administered for accountability purposes.

Similarly, states and districts should develop clear guidelines for accommodations that permit English-language learners to participate in assessments administered for accountability purposes. Especially important are clear decision rules for determining the level of English language proficiency at which English-language learners should be expected to participate exclusively in English-language assessments. English-language learners should be exempted from assessments only when there is evidence that the assessment, even with accommodations, cannot measure the knowledge or skill of particular students or groups of students.

In an education improvement system, data from assessments provide information that teachers and administrators can use to revise their instructional program to enable students to reach challenging standards. For that reason, assessment results should be reported so that they indicate the status of student performance against standards. To ensure accuracy, reports of student performance should include measures of statistical uncertainty, such as a confidence interval or the probability of misclassification. States, districts, and schools should disaggregate data to ensure that schools will be accountable for the progress of all children, especially those with the greatest educational needs.

Monitoring the Conditions of Instruction

The theory of action of the basic standards-based reform model suggests that, armed with data on how students perform against standards, schools will make the instructional changes needed to improve performance. Research on early implementation of standards-based systems shows, however, that many schools lack an understanding of the changes that are needed and lack the capacity to make them. The link between assessment and instruction needs to be made strong and explicit.

One way to forge such a link is by monitoring the conditions of instruction and instructional support. Information about the effects of instructional change—particularly student work that shows the quality of assignments—sends a strong signal about the kinds of changes needed and the impact of new practices. In addition, such information serves as "leading indicators" of performance.

Schools and districts should monitor the conditions of instruction—the curriculum and instructional practices of teachers—to determine if students are exposed to teaching that would enable them to achieve the standards they are expected to meet. Schools should use such information to demand support for instructional improvement in every classroom, and districts should use the information to provide such support.

Districts should also use data on the conditions of instruction, along with results from student assessments, to design their professional development program.

Accountability

Accountability is one of the most prominent issues in education policy today. Accountability mechanisms create incentives for educators to focus on important outcomes. They also provide a means for allocating resources, such as instructional assistance, to schools in which performance measures indicate problems.

In designing accountability mechanisms, states and districts must first determine an adequate level of progress for schools. Measures of adequate yearly progress should include a range of indicators, including indicators of instructional quality as well as student outcomes. In addition, the criterion for adequate yearly progress should be based on evidence from the highest-performing schools with significant proportions of disadvantaged students.

Accountability should follow responsibility: teachers and administrators—individually and collectively—should be held accountable for their part in improving student performance. Teachers and administrators should be held accountable for the progress of their students. Districts and states should be held accountable for the professional development and support they provide teachers and schools to enable students to reach high standards.

Accountability provides a way to focus assistance to schools. Assistance should be aimed at strengthening schools' capacity for educating all students to high standards and to building the internal accountability within schools. Without developing school capacity, accountability leads to inappropriate practices, such as efforts to increase test scores without improving student learning.

Education improvement systems continually change, based on new knowledge and new circumstances. States and districts should continually monitor and review their systems to determine where improvements are needed and make the changes necessary to improve educational opportunities for all children, and particularly for the disadvantaged children Title I was established to support.

CHAPTER 1

Introduction

Title I of the Elementary and Secondary Education Act is the largest federal effort in precollegiate education. Created in 1965, when the federal government for the first time agreed to provide aid to elementary and secondary schools, the program was designed to level the playing field for disadvantaged students by providing financial assistance to schools to compensate for the advantages enjoyed at schools with students from more affluent families. Now with an annual budget of approximately $8 billion—a fourth of the U.S. Department of Education's total annual budget—the program reaches more than 11 million students in two-thirds of all elementary schools and more than a fourth of all secondary schools.

Although Title I is large by federal standards, the program in fact represents a tiny fraction of the nearly $300 billion spent each year on precollegiate education. Nevertheless, Title I (the program was called Chapter 1 between 1981 and 1994) has exerted a powerful influence on schools and school districts. This is particularly true in the area of testing. From its inception, Title I required the use of "appropriate objective measures of educational achievement" in order to ensure that the program was achieving its goal of reducing the achievement gap between low-income and higher-income students. In carrying out this requirement, states and school districts, for the most part, used standardized norm-referenced tests to measure the achievement of eligible students—both to determine eligibility and to measure gains. As a result, Title I increased dramatically the number of tests that states and districts administered; one district administrator estimated that the Title I requirements doubled the amount of testing in the district (Office of Technology Assessment, 1992). Increasingly, the tests that districts used to report to Title I officials became the basis of the district's testing program. In that way, the relatively modest federal investment proved to be a lever that moved practice in nearly every school in the country.

As a number of reports and studies have concluded, however, this influence was not altogether beneficial. For one thing, despite the dollars spent and the testing requirements imposed, the achievement gap between disadvantaged and more advantaged students persists. In fact, the most extensive study of the program found that Title I failed even to narrow the achievement gap. In the final report of that study, known as Prospects, Puma et. al. (1997) found that "where students started out relative to their classmates is where they ended up in later grades." The researchers caution, however, that this finding does not indicate that Title I was a failure, particularly since funds did reach their intended beneficiaries. It may be, they point out, that the gap would have widened further if not for Title I assistance.

As a number of commentators have suggested, the testing requirements may have contributed to the failure to produce achievement gains for low-income students. According to the Advisory Commission on Testing in Chapter 1 (1993:13), "There is evidence that Chapter 1 testing procedures may indeed be promoting undesirable instructional practices, limiting the kinds of learning experiences to which students are exposed, or reinforcing outmoded ways of teaching disadvantaged students." In large part, the questionable testing practices came about in response to federal requirements. In particular, the federal government required schools to test Title I students using nationally normed tests, which compare students' performance to that of a nationally representative norming group, in order to permit comparisons across states and districts. But while these tests may provide information that is useful for program monitoring, they are less useful for providing information about students' knowledge and skills that would help guide instruction. And, because Title I was intended as a compensatory education program, the tests usually measured basic skills only, to provide information on how students participating in the program fared on such tasks. The Advisory Commission found, however, that the reliance on norm-referenced tests of basic skills to produce national data on student achievement encouraged schools and teachers to narrow the curriculum to the material tested and to "spend undue time teaching test-taking skills or low-level basic skills, rather than challenging content" (p. 13).

In response to such concerns, the Congress revamped the Title I law substantially in 1994: perhaps the most far-reaching changes were in the assessment arena. Specifically, the law required states to develop challenging standards for student performance and assessments that measure student performance against the standards. Significantly, the law states that the standards and assessments are expected to be the same for all students, regardless of whether they are eligible for Title I. Thus for the first time, the 1994 statute enshrines into law the principle that Title I students are to be held to the same standards as all other students.

These changes did not come about in a vacuum. To be sure, they represented a response to the well-documented shortcomings of the Title I program as it existed for its first 30 years. But the new law also fit squarely within the reform context of the early 1990s. Specifically, the law's focus on standards for student performance, and its premise that all students are expected to meet challenging standards, conformed to the emphasis in the reform movement on standards as the fulcrum of redesigned schools and school systems. Many of the most prominent reform efforts of the era, notably the Kentucky Education Reform Act, the most sweeping statewide reform statute in history, share this focus on standards and are considered examples of "standards-based reform." This general category refers to the idea of creating high standards for all students, measuring student performance against such standards, giving schools flexibility in how they design curriculum and instruction to enable students to meet the standards, and holding schools strictly accountable for attaining the standards. By requiring states to develop standards for student performance—the same challenging standards for all students—and to develop assessments linked to the standards, the Title I law in effect required states to adopt standards-based reform.

Moreover, the 1994 Title I statute also reflected the ferment in testing and assessment that has churned up the field since the mid-1980s. At that time, as state testing mandates increased and testing became more prevalent and more prominent in schools, critics became more vocal. Like the critics who focused specifically on Title I testing, including the Advisory Commission cited above, the testing critics charged that the growing use of testing with high stakes attached narrowed the curriculum and encouraged schools to emphasize low-level skills and knowledge at the expense of more challenging abilities. In place of such tests, reformers argued for so-called performance-based assessments, which ask students to demonstrate their knowledge and skill by performing a task, such as writing an essay, completing a science experiment, or explaining their solution to a mathematics problem. The reformers also argued for reporting assessment results based on how well a student performed against expectations for achievement, rather than a comparison with other students' performance.

The Title I law fit into this assessment reform movement by requiring tests that measure performance against standards, rather than those that compare student performance with that of other students. In addition, the law explicitly mandates that states use multiple, up-to-date measures of student performance, thus enshrining in law the demand for reform in assessment. In addition, the law also requires states to:

• Use assessments for purposes for which they are valid and reliable and ensure that such assessments are consistent with relevant, nationally recognized professional and technical standards;

- Administer assessments at least once between grades 3 and 5, and again between grades 6 and 9 and grades 10 and 12;
- Provide disaggregated achievement data that indicate the performance of students by gender, race, income, and other categories;
- Establish at least two levels of achievement, proficient and advanced, and indicate the proportion of students who attain each level, as well as a third level of performance, partially proficient, to provide information about the progress of lower-performing children toward reaching to the proficient and advanced levels;
- Determine what constitutes "adequate yearly progress" on the new assessments and hold schools and districts accountable for meeting such targets.

The record of states in implementing the new law show that the 1994 statute poses a substantial challenge. Although nearly every state has adopted content standards, as the law requires, reviews of such standards show that their rigor and usefulness vary widely (American Federation of Teachers, 1998; Council for Basic Education, 1998; Fordham Foundation, 1998). In addition, only 21 states and Puerto Rico adopted performance standards by the law's deadline of spring 1998; the rest received waivers to allow them more time.

Although the law's requirements for assessments and accountability do not take effect until 2000-2001, the plans that states have developed for such measures suggest that they may fall short of the law's intent. For example, many states have failed to indicate that they will include students with disabilities and English-language learners in their assessments, despite the law's requirements that they do so. Others have created accountability mechanisms that do not necessarily encourage schools to focus attention on poor and disadvantaged students (Citizens' Commission on Civil Rights, 1998; Chun and Goertz, 1999).

In part because of the uneven progress in implementing the statute, several commentators have begun the debate over the 1999 reauthorization of the Elementary and Secondary Education Act by suggesting that it is time to rethink Title I's purpose and to rewrite the law in dramatic ways. Some critics, contending that the law has failed in its attempt to raise the academic performance of poor children, have argued that the federal government should scrap most of its rules and send money to states with few strings attached, while holding states accountable for results (Finn et al., 1999; Ravitch, 1999). Others maintain that under Title I the federal government has been too lax and has allowed states to support reforms that were ineffective or even harmful; they argue that Title I funds should be directed at efforts that have been shown to improve schooling for disadvantaged children (Orfield, 1999). Still others note that the law is not yet fully in place, but that its principles are sound and could show promise if implemented effectively (Independent Review Panel, 1999).

The purpose of this report is not to recommend a plan for the reauthorization of Title I. The Committee on Title I Testing and Assessment was not asked to critique the law nor to evaluate its implementation. The committee was asked to bring to bear our analysis of the evidence and our experience in schools, school districts, and states to help states and districts implement the statute in a way that will be effective for the disadvantaged students Title I is intended to benefit.

THE COMMITTEE'S APPROACH

The Committee on Title I Testing and Assessment was charged with assessing research on the use of testing and assessment for accountability purposes, examining the experience of states and districts in this domain, and developing a "decision framework that incorporates technical quality, effects on teaching and learning, costs and benefits, fairness, and other criteria for evaluating assessment strategies." Our goal was to produce a practical guide for states and districts to use in developing the systems they were creating under the Title I law.

The committee went about its task in a number of ways. First, we reviewed available evidence from research on assessment, accountability, and standards-based reform. However, we recognized that in many areas the evidentiary base was slim. Standards-based reform is a new idea, and few places have put all the pieces in place, and even fewer have put them in place long enough to enable scholars to observe their effects. Therefore, we supplemented our review of the research with evidence from our own observations and reports from the field. Many committee members are practitioners, whose daily work is to develop and implement assessments and accountability mechanisms. Other members are in classrooms regularly, helping and observing teachers and administrators as they implement standards-based reform. The knowledge gleaned from these observations helped inform our work.

In addition, the committee also sought testimony from educators in leading-edge states and districts, who described for the committee their efforts. This testimony helped the committee understand not only the effects of assessment and accountability, but also the practical challenges involved in putting in place a system constrained by cost and political demands.

As we studied the research, examined our own experiences, and listened to the testimony, the committee kept in mind three underlying principles. First, the committee agreed that the purpose of assessment and accountability is to contribute to and support high levels of student learning. We recognized that there are many ways to respond to the law's requirements, and some evidence suggests that at least some states fell well short of the law's goals even as they complied with its mandates (Citizens' Commission on Civil Rights, 1998). Yet, in the committee's view, the potential educational power of assessment and accountability far outweighs the bureaucratic purposes of such instruments, particularly for those who have been historically poorly served by the education system. We therefore used as a yardstick a simple measure: whether a state's decision would help improve student learning and reduce the achievement gap. Simple compliance with the law was not enough.

Second, the committee agreed that the education improvement system, of which assessment and accountability are key components, should be conceived of and implemented as just that—a *system*. That is, the system should consist of a number of components, at various levels (classroom, school, school district, and state), each of which plays a role in measuring and contributing to student learning, yet which are interrelated, not separate from one another. Applying this principle, one might view one component—for example, a state testing program—that by itself falls short, as appropriate in a system that also includes components that complement it.

Third, the committee agreed that a hallmark of the state and district systems should be continuous improvement at all levels—for students, for teachers and administrators, and for the system itself. Improvement for students is obvious; as noted above, it is the reason for the system. Improvement for teachers and administrators is also a necessary part of the system. Although the role of professional development was not formally part of the committee's charge, the committee found it impossible to discuss assessment without addressing the role of enhancing the knowledge and skills of teachers. High student performance depends on high-quality instruction, and building the capacity of teachers and administrators is at least as much a necessary condition of educational improvement as establishing standards or putting in place accountability mechanisms.

Improvement for the system itself is also essential. Assessments and accountability schemes change constantly, despite the best-laid plans of educators and blue-ribbon panels. Legislators, responding to teachers, parents, and other constituents, frequently mandate adjustments, from adding multiple-choice components to requiring individual student reports. And administrators change programs as data come in that show the effects of the system on students and schools. Although the Title I statute calls the assessments that are to be put in place by 2000-2001 "final," these assessments are likely to undergo numerous rounds of revision, even if the structure of the education improvement system remains in place.

Moreover, as noted above, the effects of the components of a standards-based system are not completely certain. Many of the systems the committee studied are relatively new or still in some cases under development, and their full impact on students, particularly disadvantaged students, remains to be seen. Therefore, states and districts need to monitor their improvement systems continually, to ensure that they are achieving their desired goals.

For these and other reasons, the committee developed criteria not for the one best system—which does not exist—but for systems that are continually changing and adapting to new knowledge and new circumstances. In this way, the committee's framework is appropriate for states and districts just starting out on redesigning their education improvement system, as well as for states and districts that have had redesigned systems in place for several years.

The committee also recognized that each state and district must develop its own system to meet local circumstances. The committee did not intend to propose a blueprint that all states and districts should adopt. Rather, our guidelines are intended to be used as yardsticks against which states and districts can measure their own judgments. Moreover, we recognize that building effective education improvement systems is hard work, particularly in the charged political environments in which states and school districts operate. We would never presume that policy makers or administrators could simply implement complex systems with a wave of the hand, much less carry through with the even harder work of building the capacity of schools to educate all students to high levels.

ORGANIZATION OF THIS REPORT

To carry out its charge to provide guidance to state and district officials responsible for making decisions about appropriate assessment and accountability systems to meet the requirements of the Title I law, the committee has conceived of this report as a *guide*. That is, it was designed to be useful as well as informative. To that end, we have organized the report so that our readers can walk through the various components of the system and consider a set of questions that state and district leaders should ask themselves as they develop their systems. We identify what we consider the key criteria for each component. And we include examples of states and districts that have applied these criteria in different ways.

This approach is intended to accomplish two goals. First, we present what our review of the research and our experience show are the basic principles beneath an effective system, allowing state and district officials to measure their own approaches against our criteria. Second, we present examples to show that there are many ways of applying these criteria; we do not want to suggest at any point that there is one right way to do this. In addition, we do not want to suggest that these examples represent ideal solutions to the challenges states and districts face. Some of these examples do not completely meet our criteria, and we indicate this in introducing them. Some examples remain controversial and deserve continuing study; a future edition of this guide might include a different set of examples.

Before turning to the criteria, however, we need to examine the entire system. In Chapter 2, we consider and critique the theory of action behind the Title I law and the various attempts at standards-based reform. We then expand on the theory of action to reflect our analysis of effective reform.

In Chapter 3, we begin to lay out the components of the system by examining the issue of standards. In Chapter 4, we discuss assessments, including assessments for young children and for special populations, as well as reporting and disaggregating assessment results. In Chapter 5, we consider systems for monitoring the conditions of instruction at the school level and professional development at the district level. In Chapter 6, we examine ways to measure adequate progress of schools toward standards, and in Chapter 7 we discuss accountability.

CHAPTER 2

Toward a Theory of Action

The task of the Committee on Title I Testing and Assessment was to develop a guide for states and districts to assist them in implementing the Title I statute. This guide includes criteria for the components of an effective education improvement system, along with examples of ways states and districts have applied these criteria. But to understand the committee's point of view, we need first to present the big picture—the "theory of action" that animates the entire system.

The 1994 law that reauthorized Title I of the Elementary and Secondary Education Act drew on a powerful strain of education thinking that has grown increasingly prominent in the past decade. Beginning with the publication of the National Council of Teachers of Mathematics Standards in 1989, and accelerating after the establishment a year later of the national education goals, educators and policy makers have increasingly focused on standards for student performance as the centerpiece of education reform; indeed, the idea has since acquired the name "standards-based reform." The Title I statute fits squarely within that tradition.

Generally, the idea of standards-based reform states that, if states set high standards for student performance, develop assessments that measure student performance against the standards, give schools the flexibility they need to change curriculum, instruction, and school organization to enable their students to meet the standards, and hold schools strictly accountable for meeting performance standards, then student achievement will rise.

This idea is not unique to education. A number of businesses have implemented similar principles and have won acclaim as high-performing organizations. The Saturn Corporation, for example, which was created by General Motors and the United Auto Workers during the steep slump in the domestic automobile industry, has attracted considerable attention for its innovative standards-based structure. At Saturn, the company sets high goals for performance (e.g., a standard of zero defects), measures performance regularly, and gives extraordinary authority to teams of workers, including line workers, while linking their pay and job security to performance.

Likewise, a number of public-sector agencies are "reinventing government" by adopting similar principles (Osborne and Gaebler, 1993).

In education, the idea of standards-based reform grew in part out of the same notions that drove the reforms in business and government, but also out of a critique of previous education reform efforts, particularly the experience with Title I and Chapter 1. Yet despite the prominence of standards-based reform in the policy debate, there are few examples of districts or states that have put the entire standards-based puzzle together, much less achieved success through it. Some evidence is beginning to gather. Grissmer and Flanagan (1998), for example, found that North Carolina and Texas have produced gains in student performance through the implementation of standards-based systems. Other evidence comes from Europe and Asia, where national systems of education have produced curriculum guides and related assessments, and where many countries outperform the United States on international assessments (Schmidt et al., 1998).

In large part, the limited body of evidence in this country reflects the complexity of the concept. It requires substantial changes in a number of major interlocking dimensions, and education policy seldom occurs in such a systematic fashion. Moreover, it poses the technical challenge of creating new instruments and systems, all of which are exceedingly controversial and costly, in the center of a highly charged political arena.

THE STANDARDS-BASED REFORM MODEL

The theory of action of standards-based reform rests on four major components: standards, assessments, flexibility, and accountability. It is represented graphically in Figure 2-1.

Setting Standards. As its name suggests, standards-based reform rests primarily on standards for student performance. The standards should be clear,

FIGURE 2-1 Model of the theory of action of standards-based reform

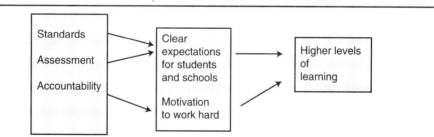

high, and the same for all students. Reformers argue that setting clear, high standards for all students will help improve their performance by giving students, parents, and teachers a vivid picture of what good work looks like and what they have to do to produce it.

Aligning Assessments. Assessments are linked to standards so closely in discussions of standards-based reform that the two are often referred to almost as one word: "standardsandassessments." But the link is important. Assessments make the standards concrete by providing students with opportunities to demonstrate the knowledge and skills the standards call for. At the same time, they serve as a means by which students, parents, teachers, and administrators can know the extent to which students are meeting the standards.

Providing Flexibility. For years, educators have complained that the plethora of rules associated with Title I have hamstrung their efforts to redesign their instructional programs and have forced them to use questionable practices in order to comply with statutory mandates. For example, administrators say, schools have pulled Title I students out of their regular classrooms in order to provide specialized instruction for them, even though research suggests that such programs have been implemented in ineffective ways, because schools were required to demonstrate that they were in fact providing compensatory education services to eligible children.

Standards-based reform changes the rules of the game by measuring performance against standards rather than compliance with procedures. Policy makers will know if their money is spent well if student performance improves, not if schools follow rules faithfully. Thus, lawmakers can relax rules that mandate how schools must go about their jobs. And that, in turn, will help improve student performance, reformers say, by reducing the impediments schools now face in designing instructional programs appropriate for their student populations.

Requiring Accountability. Accountability is the flip side of the coin of flexibility. In exchange for the freedom to design instructional programs according to local needs, schools in standards-based systems are no longer held accountable for following rules and procedures and making sure that funds are spent as intended. Rather, they are accountable for results—for ensuring that student learning improves.

Holding schools accountable for results serves a number of purposes. Accountability helps keep educators' "eyes on the prize," reducing the possibility that they will spend their time on issues less directly related to improving student performance. On the other hand, accountability creates an incentive for teachers and administrators at all levels to use standards to guide curricular and instructional decisions, and to use assessment results to diagnose problems and suggest ways to improve. On the other hand, holding schools accountable for some other set of instructional goals will encourage schools to focus on those goals, rather than the standards, regardless of how compelling the standards may be.

Although each of these elements—standards, assessments, flexibility, and accountability—is itself complex and challenging to administer, the essence of standards-based reform is the idea that states must implement all of them. Reformers argue that previous education reforms failed because they were piecemeal; they addressed one aspect of the system while leaving the rest untouched, and failed to address the core of schooling. Without a comprehensive change, standards-based reform will suffer the same fate.

How, then, to implement such a massive change? The Title I statute lays out a precise schedule for implementing standards-based reform. The law's sequence is as follows: flexibility, standards, assessments, and accountability.

Not all states and districts have followed this linear sequence. In some places, political exigencies have led policy makers to put in place accountability measures before standards and assessments were revised. Others followed a different approach because of a different conception of how to achieve change. For example, Community District 2 in New York City started with a vision of teaching and learning and invested heavily in developing teachers' knowledge and skills to be able to realize the vision. They held teachers and administrators accountable for the quality of instruction and made sure that everyone in the system, from teachers all the way to the deputy superintendent, knows the quality of the staff, the quality of teaching, and the quality of student work in each school. Only after years of developing teachers' abilities—and after rising from 16th to 2nd among New York City districts in performance on conventional tests—did the district adopt standards and a testing system that they believed reflected their instructional goals (Elmore and Burney, 1998).

Regardless of the approach, the expectation is the same: comprehensive standards-based reform systems will result in students' meeting high standards for performance.

THE THEORY IN PRACTICE

In a study conducted for the National Education Goals Panel, David Grissmer and Ann Flanagan (1998) examined two states that registered large gains in student performance in mathematics and reading in the 1990s, North Carolina and Texas. They found that many of the factors often associated with improved student performance—increases in education spending, reductions in class size, changes in the student population—did not explain the results in the two states they studied. Rather, they suggested, what the two states had in common were a set of statewide policies that coincided with the increases in test scores. These policies were: statewide academic standards, by grade, for clear teaching objectives, holding all students to the same standards, statewide assessments closely linked to the standards, accountability systems with consequences for results, increasing local flexibility for administrators and teachers, computerized feedback systems and data for continuous improvement, shifting resources to schools with more disadvantaged students, and an infrastructure to sustain reform. These policies were, in short, the main elements of standards-based reform.

Grissmer and Flanagan found few data to show how teachers and administrators in North Carolina and Texas changed their practices in ways that produced higher test scores. "But," they conclude, "it appears to be the changed design of the organizational environment and competitive incentive structure which is responsible for teachers and administrators finding creative ways to foster higher achievement in their students" (p. 21).

Other evidence suggests that standards-based reform can be effective when district policies to establish standards-based assessments and accountability mechanisms are coupled with strategies for instructional improvement. Case studies of reform efforts in San Antonio, Philadelphia, and Memphis, for example, show that these districts achieved gains after instituting standards-based accountability systems and assistance to local schools to revise curricular and instructional practices (Citizens' Commission on Civil Rights, 1998).

Other studies suggest that if the link between standards-based policies at the state and district levels and instructional improvement at the school level is not clear-cut, then higher student performance may not result. In these instances, the theory of standards-based reform may not work as designed.

For example, an examination of district policies that call for "reconstitution" of failing schools (breaking up the faculty and staff and rebuilding it from the ground up) found that schools threatened with severe penalties are not changing their instructional practices in fundamental ways. Instead, they seem to focus on short-term gains in test scores, rather than deep improvements in student learning (O'Day, in press).

Another study of 20 schools found that the internal accountability within schools—that is, teachers' collective responsibility for improving student learning and for making the changes necessary to bring such improvements about— varies widely (Abelmann and Elmore, 1999). When such internal accountability is weak, the willingness of teachers to change their practice in fundamental ways to respond to external accountability pressures may be lacking.

These studies and observations from our own experience have led the committee to call into question some of the assumptions that appear to be embedded in the theory of action underlying the standards-based reform model in general and the Title I law in particular. Chief among these assumptions is the idea that teachers would institute effective practices if they had both the freedom and the motivation to do so. Relaxing rules would provide the freedom; holding schools accountable for results would provide the motivation.

The committee found that this idea may be overoptimistic. First, it assumes that teachers—indeed, the education profession generally—know enough about what it takes to educate all children to challenging standards of performance. The experience since 1994 suggests that, although some schools and communities are showing success, their practices are not widely shared, and knowledge about how to implement effective instructional strategies to help all students learn to challenging standards is also largely unknown.

Second, implicit in the theory is the notion that motivated teachers would seek guidance about improving instruction and districts would provide the support teachers need, largely by making more widely available the existing array of professional development opportunities. Recent research suggests, however, that the amount and kind of professional development is inadequate to meet teachers' needs, and that teachers continue to feel unprepared to teach all students to challenging standards (National Center for Education Statistics, 1999; National Partnership for Excellence and Accountability in Teaching, 1999).

As a result of our examination of the theory of action, the committee concludes that the theory needs to be expanded to make explicit the link between standards, assessments, accountability, *instruction*, and learning. In our view, standards-based policies can affect student learning only if they are tied directly to efforts to build the capacity of teachers and administrators to improve instruction.

AN EXPANDED THEORY

What would such a system look like? In our view, the focus would be on *teaching and learning*, and the theory of action revolves around the links between all the elements and instruction. We call the expanded system an "education improvement system," and it is represented graphically in Figure 2-2.

The theory of action behind an education improvement system relies on information and responsibility. Everyone—students, parents, teachers, principals, district administrators, state officials, and policy makers at the district, state, and federal levels—knows what it is expected, what they will be measured on, and what the results imply for what they should do next. Those directly responsible for raising student performance—teachers and schools—have access to high-quality information about performance and about the effects of their instruc-

FIGURE 2-2 Expanded model of the theory of action of standards-based reform: An education improvement system

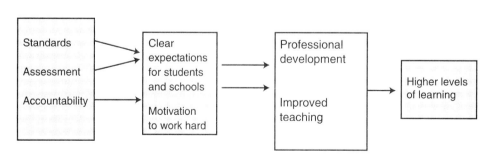

tional practices. They are then responsible for using this information to adjust their practices and seek support for additional resources for improvement.

But others have responsibilities as well, since student performance depends on the capacity of teachers and administrators to deliver high-quality instruction. Therefore, the education improvement system also provides information on the progress of efforts to develop instructional capacity. In all cases, the information the system provides is transparent—that is, it shows results and suggests remedies. In addition, the information provides a means for states and districts to monitor the effects of their changes and make course corrections when warranted.

As with the conventional model, the theory of action for education improvement systems is based on the idea that a number of components work hand in hand. States and districts can develop these components in any order; what matters is coherence among the components.

The components of an education improvement system are: standards, assessments, indicators of the conditions of instruction, and accountability.

Standards. As with standards-based reform, challenging standards for student performance drive instructionally valid standards-based systems. Content standards set expectations for learning for all students, and performance standards are the benchmarks against which progress is gauged. Performance standards also provide instructional guidance by offering clear ideas of classroom strategies to enable students to reach the standards.

Assessments. Assessments provide information on progress toward the standards, but they do so in different ways for different constituencies. Assessments serve a number of purposes—guiding instructional decisions, monitoring progress, holding schools and districts accountable. Classroom assessments provide frequent and detailed information about individual student strengths and weaknesses, district assessments monitor school progress toward standards, and state assessments provide data for use in accountability systems.

School reports consist of a range of measures—which include indicators of instructional practices, as well as student work and test scores—that provide a complete picture of performance. The reports indicate the performance of groups of students within the school or district; overall average scores may be misleading.

Not all assessments are equally capable of providing useful information. The most informative measures are ones that respond to instructional changes aimed at teaching toward the standards. Such measures inform students, teachers, and parents about the effects of instruction and suggest directions for improvement.

The array of assessments include assessments that are appropriate for young children, as well as assessments that accurately and validly measure the achievement of students with disabilities and those with limited English proficiency.

Indicators of the Conditions of Instruction. The link between instructional practice and student performance suggests the need to collect information on the conditions of instruction to which students are exposed, in addition to the student outcome measures used in the assessment system. Such indicators serve as "leading" indicators of school progress and suggest needed areas of improvement. They also could point out possible inequalities.

Measures of instructional practice at the district level also indicate the extent to which districts are fulfilling their role in building local capacity to improve instruction and student performance.

Accountability. Accountability creates an incentive for students, teachers, and administrators to focus their attention on the standards. It also closes the loop in the system by providing an explicit link to instructional improvement; rather than hit the hammer harder, administrators provide assistance where the accountability measures suggest it is needed, and direct teachers' and school administrators' attention to the standards.

Such a system is never "complete." States and districts need to examine each component and the system as a whole, continually, to determine the extent to which it is achieving the goal of improving teaching and learning. In the following chapters we outline the criteria for each of the components.

CHAPTER 3

Standards for
Student Performance

As the name implies, standards-based reform places standards at the heart of the system. The goal is to focus the attention of everyone in the system on what students are expected to learn—the results schooling is expected to achieve—rather than on the resources or effort put into the system. Moreover, standards-based systems are intended to set common learning expectations for all students, regardless of background or where they happen to attend school.

For these reasons, standards-based reform represents a substantial shift from the practice that has prevailed in American education, and particularly the experience in Title I. For much of its existence, the emphasis in Title I was on compliance with rules and procedures, rather than student learning. The program was typically regarded as an add-on to the regular instructional program, and students were often pulled out of their regular classrooms for Title I instruction. This occurred in large part so that administrators could ensure that the resources reached the intended beneficiaries.

To be sure, the program, particularly after the 1988 reauthorization, required schools to demonstrate improvements in student learning. But schools merely had to show that students achieved more than they did before, not that they reached designated levels of academic performance. And, as some commentators noted, students who registered large gains ended up ineligible for the program, thus providing a perverse incentive for schools not to increase student achievement. A standards-based system, by contrast, is aimed not at comparing the performance of poor children with that of other poor children, but at setting a target for all children—poor as well as affluent—and determining whether they are on the way toward reaching it.

The emphasis in the standards movement on *all* students is also a departure from past practice. As a number of studies have shown, the curriculum, instructional practice, and, above all, the expectations for student achievement differ sharply among schools. Simply put, the standards are higher in schools with more affluent students. As Puma et. al. (1997) found in their extensive study of the program (then Chapter 1), an A in a high-poverty school was the equivalent of a C in a low-poverty school.

Standards are intended to change that practice by setting out a body of knowledge and skills that are essential for all students to learn and expecting all students to learn it. The explicit intention of the reformers was to set challenging standards for all students.

CONTENT STANDARDS

indings

Research on standards and standards-based systems specifies two types of standards: content standards and performance standards. Both are required by the Title I statute.

Content standards spell out what students should know and be able to do in core subjects. They indicate, for example, the topics and skills that should be taught at various grade levels or grade spans. At the national level, the mathematics standards developed by the National Council of Teachers of Mathematics and the science standards developed by the National Research Council (NRC) are examples of content standards. For example, the NRC's National Science Education Standards for physical science state that, at grades K-4, "all students should develop an understanding of properties of objects and materials; position and motion of objects; [and] light, heat, electricity, and magnetism." In grades 5-8, "all students should develop an understanding of properties and changes of properties in matter; motions and forces; [and] transfer of energy." In grades 9-12, "all students should develop an understanding of structure of atoms; structure and properties of matter; chemical reactions; motions and forces; conservation of energy and increase in disorder; [and] interactions of energy and matter" (National Research Council, 1996: 123, 149, 176).

In addition to the standards proposed by national groups, nearly all states have developed content standards in core subjects. These standards vary widely, however. Some states set standards for grade clusters, like the National Science Education Standards, while others set standards for each grade. Some focus on a few big ideas, while others are quite extensive.

The purpose of content standards is to guide instruction by providing a common focus for policy and practice (Ravitch, 1995). At the policy level, they provide guidelines for the development of assessments, instructional materials, and professional development opportunities, thus helping to steer teachers' decisions about what to teach. In addition, the standards documents themselves set common expectations for all classrooms and provide a yardstick for school and district staffs to use in evaluating and changing their curricula or instructional programs.

Because content standards represent a community's expectations for all children, setting content standards is a political process. In most cases, standards have been set by groups of subject-matter experts, educators, representatives of the public, and public officials, usually meeting in the public eye. The public process is aimed at ensuring that the result earns broad approval.

In practice, though, this public effort at times has been hotly contentious. Different groups come into the process with different goals for students. For example, some want to emphasize students' readiness for the workplace; others place a higher priority on the knowledge and skills young people need for effective citizenship; others stress students' need to understand an increasingly multicultural society.

Largely as a result of these often-raucous debates, the products of these efforts vary widely. Some standards are highly specific, spelling out in detail the content knowledge students should demonstrate, whereas others are more general—or vague, as critics contend. The degree to which the standards are "challenging" also varies, with some states demanding much more of their students than others.

Several organizations have evaluated the state standards, in order to provide some independent determination of the quality of the documents (American Federation of Teachers, 1998; Council for Basic Education, 1998; Fordham Foundation, 1998; Wixson and Dutro, 1998). However, the ratings of these organizations vary, depending on the criteria they use to assess standards. The American Federation of Teachers, for example, focused on clarity and specificity, whereas the Council for Basic Education emphasized "rigor." As a result, to take one case, Virginia's English standards were rated as "exemplary" by the American Federation of Teachers, yet earned a B-minus from the Council for Basic Education.

The standards also vary in the degree to which they guide policy and practice. On the one hand, standards that are considered general can be assessed in many ways, but it is difficult to make a valid inference about student performance against standards that can be interpreted so broadly. At the same time, as one study of nine states found, state standards that were considered general had little influence on instruction, since teachers can interpret the standards idiosyncratically. Standards that are specific, in contrast, tend to yield similar interpretations by all teachers, and thus can be implemented more easily. However, states varied in the extent to which they provided assistance to local educators to implement standards (Massell et al., 1997). The role of states and districts in helping schools implement standards is considered in Chapter 5.

On the other hand, standards that are too numerous provide little guidance to either assessment designers or local educators, because they contain too many topics and skills for assessment designers to include on assessments or for teachers to teach in a school year. Assessments that attempt to measure an extensive set of detailed standards either omit standards or measure some with a handful of items, threatening the reliability and validity of the interpretations from the assessment. Teachers face a similar dilemma. An analysis of standards documents by the Mid-Continent Regional Educational Laboratory found that it would take about 15,000 classroom hours to teach adequately the content included in standards documents in 14 subject areas—a length of time that would add 9 or 10 years to a child's school career (Marzano et al., 1999). Faced with such an overwhelming task, teachers are likely to select the standards they choose to teach, and the purpose of standards as a guiding document will get lost.

Teachers also face challenges in districts that have adopted their own sets of standards, in addition to the standards the state has developed. Without a mechanism for determining the alignment of the district standards with the state standards, teachers have to choose whether to focus on one or the other. They are most likely either to choose which standards to teach or to focus on those reflected in a test.

In an aligned system, the state's standards become the core knowledge and skills that students are expected to demonstrate at critical junctures, and the basis for determining school progress. A district's standards would elaborate on the state's standards and provide the basis for professional development to enhance teachers' knowledge and skills in improving student learning.

ecommendations

- Content standards must be clear, parsimonious, and rigorous.
- States and districts should obtain external review for their content standards to ensure that the standards reflect a high level of clarity and rigor and an appropriate level of specificity.
- Content standards must provide clear direction to educators responsible for the design of assessments, professional development, and curriculum materials.
- Content standards must provide clear direction to teachers and administrators about what they need to teach to improve student learning.

uestions to Ask

❑ Have the standards been reviewed independently for their clarity, rigor, and parsimony?

❑ Do the standards provide clear guidance to designers of assessments, professional development programs, and curriculum materials?

❑ Do the standards provide clear guidance to teachers?

Criteria

In determining the quality of their standards, states and districts should examine them across a range of dimensions. The committee recommends using at least the following criteria:

Basis in Content. Standards are most effective as guides for instruction when they focus on the essential knowledge and skills in a subject area. Standards for student attitudes and beliefs are more difficult to build instructional programs around, more difficult to measure, and they may be inappropriate.

Cognitive Complexity. Standards challenge all students when they ask them not only to demonstrate knowledge of fundamental facts in a discipline but also to show that they can use their knowledge to analyze new situations and reason effectively.

Reasonableness. Standards are effective when students, teachers, and parents believe they are attainable with effort. Standards that are far beyond what students should be reasonably expected to achieve—asking fourth graders to analyze *Hamlet*—invite cynicism and encourage schools to try to get around them.

Focus and Parsimony. Similarly, standards are effective when they are perceived to be attainable within the constraints of classroom capacity. Standards that are too extensive and that cannot possibly be addressed in full are counterproductive.

Clarity. Standards can guide classroom practice if teachers can translate the instructional goals into instructional activities. On the one hand, standards that are vague and that lead to innumerable interpretations are less helpful. On the other hand, standards that are too detailed encourage schools to emphasize breadth at the expense of depth.

Examples

The following two examples of state standards—science standards from Connecticut (Box 3-1) and mathematics standards from North Carolina (Box 3-2)—generally meet the committee's criteria. They have both earned high marks from the three national organizations that review standards, and both provide clear guidance to assessment developers and teachers. Both also represent parsimonious choices about what is important in their respective disciplines. In the case of Connecticut, the example shows how standards were revised from an earlier, longer set, to enable assessment developers to measure student performance against them.

BOX 3-1 CONNECTICUT CONTENT STANDARDS IN SCIENCE

For grades 5-8, Connecticut has adopted 14 general performance standards in science, which are further defined by 97 more detailed standards. This broad range of content is viewed as important by curriculum experts in the state, and it is consistent with national and state priorities in science. The need for the definition of a more limited domain of content became apparent in the effort to design a state assessment to measure the progress of Connecticut students in science.

For several years, Connecticut attempted to measure science achievement against the standards with a mixed-format test, which included a performance task and both multiple-choice and open-ended items, administered to every student. Because of limits on cost and testing time, however, each year's test could thoroughly and authentically assess only a very limited sample of the state's extensive content standards. Furthermore, each year's test assessed a different sample of the state's content, creating tests that were quite variable across years. This assessment design fell short of providing the direction needed by educators in school districts. As one educator stated, "We don't know how to adjust our instruction to help our students' performance because we have no idea what will be on next year's test." Fluctuations in school district assessment results over time may reflect the variable agreement between different forms of the test and a district's curriculum more than actual differences in science achievement over time. The limited progress in statewide science performance as evidenced by the assessment results may be related to this inclusive definition of content.

Reluctant to abandon the mix of item formats and the idea of administering the test to every student, state curriculum and testing officials began to revise the test content in preparation for a new generation of Connecticut assessments. Limiting the content to be tested proved the most arduous task. Recognizing that not all content standards would be tested and that those that would be tested needed to be limited and more clearly defined, science specialists had to make difficult decisions about what are the most essential skills and knowledge Connecticut should expect all students to attain.

We provide examples showing how Connecticut officials redefined their content standards in the area of genetics and evolution. Initially, there were six specific standards within that broad category:

Educational experiences in Grades 5-8 will assure that students:

- understand that each organism carries a set of instructions (genes) for specifying the components and functions of the organism;
- explain that differences between parents and offspring can accumulate in successive generations so that descendants are very different from their ancestors;
- recognize that individual organisms with certain traits are more likely than others to survive and have offspring;
- understand that the extinction of a species occurs when the environment changes and the species is not able to adapt to the changes;
- understand that the basic idea of biological evolution is that the Earth's present-day species developed from earlier species; and

BOX 3-1 *(continued)*

- know that the many thousands of layrs of sedimentary rock provide evidence for the history of the Earth and its changing life forms.

In the revised version, there are two specific standards, which have been further clarified and limited by the points which follow them:

Genetics and Evolution

As a result of studying patterns of heredity and historical changes in life forms:

- Students understand how each organism carries a set of instructions (genes composed of DNA) for specifying the components and functions of the organism.
  — Describe how genetic materials are organized in genes and chromosomes in the cells of living organisms. (LIIA1)
  — Explain how the genetic information from both parents is mixed in the fertilized egg to produce an individual with new combinations of genes and traits. (LIIA2)
  — Explain how genes are related to inherited traits. (LIIA3)

- Students understand that the basic idea of biological evolution is that the Earth's present-day species developed from earlier species.
  — Explain how environmental changes can lead to the extinction and evolution of species. (LIIB1)
  — Describe how fossils and anatomical evidence provide support for the theory of evolution. (LIIB2)

The Connecticut State Department of Education will share with school districts the revised standards. The hope is that school districts will place the highest priority on these standards as they build science curricula, but that the content that has been excluded from the state assessment will continue to be an integral part of science education in the state. They hope further that district-level and school-level assessments will go beyond the state assessment to monitor the progress of students on a wider range of content.

Those who care deeply about science education in Connecticut are nervous about the content that will no longer be eligible for the state assessment. Some educators are concerned that what is not tested by the state will not be taught. State officials recognize the trade-offs and compromises. The hope is that this clearer definition of priorities will have a positive impact on science education in Connecticut, and that the resulting progress of students will be evident in the results of the assessment.

Source: Initial standards from *The Connecticut Framework: K-12 Curricular Goals and Standards*, 1998. Revised standards from draft test specifications, forthcoming. Connecticut State Department of Education. Used with permission.

BOX 3-2 North Carolina Content Standards in Mathematics

GRADE 4—MATHEMATICS COMPETENCY GOALS AND OBJECTIVES

Major Concepts

- Addition, subtraction, and multiplication with multi-digit numbers
- Division with single-digit divisors
- Points, lines, angles, and transformations in geometry
- Non-numeric symbols to represent quantities
- Range, median, and mode
- Bar, picture, and circle graphs; stem-and-leaf plots and line plots
- Probability
  - Students will create and solve relevant and authentic problems using appropriate technology and applying these concepts as well as those developed in previous years.

Computational Skills to Maintain

- Use counting strategies
- Add and subtract multi-digit numbers
- Read and write word names for numbers
- Addition, subtraction, multiplication facts/tables
- Identify, explain, and apply the commutative and identity properties for multiplication and addition

Number Sense, Numeration, and Numerical Operations

Goal 1: The learner will read, write, model, and compute with rational numbers.

1.01 Read and write numbers less than one million using standard and expanded notation.
1.02 Use estimation techniques in determining solutions to problems.
1.03 Model and identify the place value of each digit in a multi-digit numeral to the hundredths place.
1.04 Model, identify, and compare rational numbers (fractions and mixed numbers).
1.05 Identify and compare rational numbers in decimal form (tenths and hundredths) using models and pictures.
1.06 Relate decimals and fractions (tenths and hundredths) to each other using models and pictures.
1.07 Use models and pictures to add and subtract decimals, explaining the processes and recording results.
1.08 Use models and pictures to add and subtract rational numbers with like denominators.
1.09 Find the fractional part of a whole number using models and pictures.
1.10 Model and explain associative and distributive properties.
1.11 Memorize the division facts related to the multiplication facts/tables through 10.
1.12 Identify missing factors in multiplication facts.
1.13 Round rational numbers to the nearest whole number and justify.
1.14 Estimate solutions to problems.

BOX 3-2 *(continued)*

1.15 Multiply 2- or 3-digit numbers by 1-digit numbers or a 2-digit multiple of 10.

1.16 Divide using single-digit divisors, with and without remainders.

1.17 Use order of operations with addition, subtraction, multiplication, and division.

1.18 Solve multi-step problems; determine if there is sufficient data given, then select additional strategies including:
- make a chart or graph
- look for patterns
- make a simpler problem
- use logic
- work backwards
- break into parts.

Verify and interpret results with respect to the original problem; use calculators as appropriate. Discuss alternate methods for solution.

Spatial Sense, Measurement, and Geometry

Goal 2: The learner will demonstrate an understanding and use of the properties and relationships in geometry, and standard units of metric and customary measurement.

2.01 Identify points, lines, and angles (acute, right, and obtuse); identify in the environment.

2.02 Use manipulatives, pictorial representations, and appropriate vocabulary (e.g. sides, angles, and vertices) to identify properties of plane figures; identify in the environment.

2.03 Use manipulatives, pictorial representations, and appropriate vocabulary (e.g. faces, edges, and vertices) to identify properties of polyhedra (solid figures); identify in the environment.

2.04 Identify intersecting, parallel, and perpendicular lines and line segments and their midpoints; identify in the environment.

2.05 Recognize congruent plane figures after geometric transformations such as rotations (turns), reflections (flips), and translations (slides).

2.06 Use designs, models, and computer graphics to illustrate reflections, rotations, and translations of plane figures and record observations.

2.07 Estimate and measure length, capacity, and mass using these additional units: inches, miles, centimeters, and kilometers; milliliters, cups, and pints; kilograms and tons.

2.08 Write and solve meaningful, multi-step problems involving money, elapsed time, and temperature; verify reasonableness of answers.

2.09 Use models to develop the relationship between the total number of square units contained in a rectangle and the length and width of the figure.

2.10 Measure the perimeter of rectangles and triangles. Determine the area of rectangles and squares using grids; find areas of other regular and irregular figures using grids.

BOX 3-2 *(continued)*

Patterns, Relationships, and Functions

Goal 3: The learner will demonstrate an understanding of patterns and relationships.

3.01 Identify numerical and geometric patterns by stating their rules; extend the pattern, generalize, and make predictions.

3.02 Identify the pattern by stating the rule, extend the pattern, generalize the rule for the pattern, and make predictions when given a table of number pairs or a set of data.

3.03 Construct and order a table of values to solve problems associated with a given relationship.

3.04 Use non-numeric symbols to represent quantities in expressions, open sentences, and descriptions of relationships. Determine solutions to open sentences.

Data, Probability, and Statistics

Goal 4: The learner will demonstrate an understanding and use of graphing, probability, and data analysis.

4.01 Interpret and construct stem-and-leaf plots.

4.02 Display data in a variety of ways including circle graphs. Discuss the advantages and disadvantages of each form including ease of creation and purpose of the graph.

4.03 Collect, organize, and display data from surveys, research, and classroom experiments, including data collected over time. Include data from other disciplines such as science, physical education, social studies, and the media.

4.04 Interpret information orally and in writing from charts, tables, tallies, and graphs.

4.05 Use range, median, and mode to describe a set of data.

4.06 Plot points that represent ordered pairs of data from many different sources such as economics, science experiments, and recreational activities.

4.07 Investigate and discuss probabilities by experimenting with devices that generate random outcomes such as coins, number cubes, spinners.

4.08 Use a fraction to describe the probability of an event and report the outcome of an experiment.

Source: North Carolina Department of Public Instruction, web site accessed 6/21/99: http://www.dpi.state.nc.us/Curriculum/new_mathematics/grades/grade_4.html. Used with permission.

PERFORMANCE STANDARDS

*F*indings

In addition to content standards, performance standards are also key elements in standards-based systems. Performance standards give meaning to content standards by indicating what students must demonstrate in order to show that they have achieved the standards. As educators often say, performance standards answer the question: How good is good enough?

To provide such an answer, performance standards demand evidence from students' work: essays, mathematical problems, science experiments, and so forth (National Education Goals Panel, 1993). As the Goals Panel report notes, performance standards can be raised over time without affecting the content standards, simply by including work of higher and higher quality.

Performance standards serve an important instructional function (McLaughlin and Shepard, 1995). By illustrating in a vivid way the qualities of exemplary work, the standards can help students, parents, and teachers improve performance by providing models to emulate and guiding classroom strategies. To serve that function, performance standards include examples of student work that meet standards for proficiency; often they include, as a contrast, examples of work that represent levels of performance below proficiency.

Developing such standards first takes shared agreement on what constitutes work at each level of performance. The experience of teachers' scoring writing samples and other performance tasks demonstrates that such agreement is possible. But the development of such standards also takes time, since standards-setters need to collect examples of student work at all levels that are related to the content standards.

As described by Hansche (1998), performance standards consist of four elements. First, performance categories, or levels, identify the various levels of attainment student work reaches. Many states use terms such as "partially proficient," "proficient," and "advanced." Others use "below standard," "at standard," and "above standard," or some version of that system.

The second element of performance standards is a set of performance descriptors, which indicate the kind of knowledge and skills students at each performance category can demonstrate. Performance descriptors are generally specific to a content area; for example, a mathematics descriptor might include the type of problem students can solve (one-step or multistep) and whether the student can show multiple solutions to the problem.

The third element is perhaps the most critical: exemplars of performance at each level. These exemplars show work by students at each level of performance, and provide concrete illustrations of the knowledge and skills students at a given performance level are able to demonstrate. The exemplars can include responses to assessment tasks, papers written for classroom assignments, projects, or other examples. They often indicate the circumstances under which the work was produced, so that readers can know whether students had an opportunity to produce their work over a long period of time or to revise it.

The fourth element of performance standards is a set of decision rules that enable assessment designers and policy makers to determine whether students have attained a certain level of performance. Although the exemplars help educators determine whether a particular piece of student work reaches a given level of performance, educators also need to determine whether a collection of work—such as responses in an assessment or a school year's work—attains the desired level of proficiency. See Chapter 4 for a discussion of the problems associated with reporting assessment results in terms of levels of performance.

ecommendations

- Performance standards must include four elements: performance categories, performance descriptors, exemplars of performance in each category, and decision rules that enable educators to determine whether students have reached each category.
- Performance standards for proficiency and above should be attainable by students in a good program with effort over time.

uestions to Ask

❑ Do the standards indicate the levels of performance students should attain, descriptions of performance at each level, examples of student work at each level, and decision rules that enable educators to determine whether students have reached a given level?

❑ Is there evidence that the standards for proficiency represent a level that all students should be able to attain, with effort, over time?

❑ Do the standards include a range of work—such as timed test items, classroom assignments, and long-range projects—to show that students can meet standards in a variety of ways?

riteria

Transparency. Effective performance standards describe and model high quality. They include examples of the type of work students have to perform in order to meet the standards.

Continuous Improvement. Performance standards contribute to improved achievement when they encourage everyone to learn more and perform better. Simply getting over a hurdle is not enough.

Reasonableness. The standards for proficiency should be high and challenging for all students, but they should also represent reasonable expectations for what students should know and be able to do. People will aim for standards that represent genuine, believable targets for improvement, but standards that are too far beyond current levels of performance encourage schools to game the system or else foster cynicism. Standards-setters can demonstrate the reasonableness of the standards through existence proof—demonstrating that students have attained the standards—or through evidence that such levels are necessary for success in future education or employment.

Examples

The following examples of performance standards—from the New Standards Performance Standards (Figure 3-1) and the Teachers of English to Students of Other Languages (Figure 3-2)—generally meet the committee's criteria. They show high-quality work, describe the circumstances of the performance, and explain how they exemplify the standards.

FIGURE 3-1 A work sample and commentary illustrating the New Standards performance standards for elementary mathematics

The task

The following written prompt appeared on an examination:

In each situation below, four friends want to "share 25" as equally as possible. Show or explain how to "share 25" in each situation.

1. Four friends shared 25 balloons as equally as possible.

2. Four friends shared $25 as equally as possible.

3. Four friends shared 25 cookies as equally as possible.

Circumstances of performance

This sample of student work was produced under the following conditions:

√ alone	in a group
√ in class	as homework
with teacher feedback	with peer feedback
√ timed	opportunity for revision

This five minute task was part of a field test for the New Standards Reference Examination: Mathematics (Elementary).

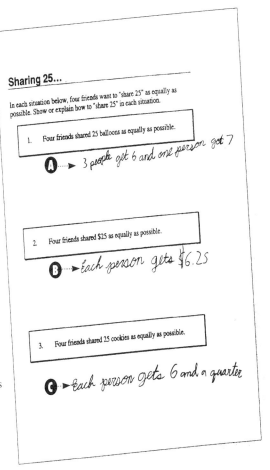

Sharing 25...

In each situation below, four friends want to "share 25" as equally as possible. Show or explain how to "share 25" in each situation.

1. Four friends shared 25 balloons as equally as possible.

A → 3 people get 6 and one person get 7

2. Four friends shared $25 as equally as possible.

B → Each person gets $6.25

3. Four friends shared 25 cookies as equally as possible.

C → Each person gets 6 and a quarter

Sources: Work sample adapted from Marilyn Burns, *Writing in Math Class,* 1995, pp. 76-82; copyright 1995 Math Solutions Publications; all rights reserved; used with permission. Commentary from *Performance Standards: Volume 1—Elementary School,* National Center on Education and the Economy, Washington, DC, 1997; used with permission.

FIGURE 3-1 *(continued)*

**This work sample illustrates
a standard-setting performance for the following
parts of the standards:**

M1 a Arithmetic and Number Concepts: Add, subtract, multiply, and divide whole numbers.

M1 c Arithmetic and Number Concepts: Estimate, approximate, round off, use landmark numbers, or use exact numbers in calculations.

M1 d Arithmetic and Number Concepts: Describe and compare quantities by using simple fractions.

M1 e Arithmetic and Number Concepts: Describe and compare quantities by using simple decimals.

M6 a Mathematical Skills and Tools: Add, subtract, multiply, and divide whole numbers correctly.

M6 d Mathematical Skills and Tools: Compute time and money.

M6 f Mathematical Skills and Tools: Use +, -, x, ÷, /, ‾�‾ , $, ¢, %, and . (decimal point) correctly in number sentences and expressions.

What the work shows

M1 a Arithmetic and Number Concepts: The student adds, subtracts, multiplies, and divides whole numbers, with and without calculators; that is:

• divides, i.e., puts things into groups, shares equally....

 A B C

• analyzes problem situations and contexts in order to figure out when to add, subtract, multiply, or divide.

A B C The student demonstrated conceptual understanding by applying arithmetic skills differently, and appropriately, in a variety of situations.

M1 c Arithmetic and Number Concepts: The student estimates, approximates, rounds off, uses landmark numbers, or uses exact numbers, as appropriate, in calculations.

A B C The correct answers demonstrate rounding off or use of exact number, as appropriate, in each situation.

M1 d Arithmetic and Number Concepts: The student describes and compares quantities by using concrete and real world models of simple fractions; that is:

• finds simple parts of wholes....

B C

M1 e Arithmetic and Number Concepts: The student describes and compares quantities by using simple decimals; that is:

• adds, subtracts, multiplies, and divides money amounts....

B

M6 a Mathematical Skills and Tools: The student adds, subtracts, multiplies, and divides whole numbers correctly....

 A B C

M6 d Mathematical Skills and Tools: The student computes...money (in dollars and cents).

B

M6 f Mathematical Skills and Tools: The student uses...$...and . (decimal point) correctly....

 B

GOAL 2, STANDARD 2

To use English to achieve academically in all content areas: Students will use English to obtain, process, construct, and provide subject matter information in spoken and written form

Descriptors

- comparing and contrasting information
- persuading, arguing, negotiating, evaluating, and justifying
- listening to, speaking, reading, and writing about subject matter information
- gathering information orally and in writing
- retelling information
- selecting, connecting, and explaining information
- analyzing, synthesizing, and inferring from information
- responding to the work of peers and others
- representing information visually and interpreting information presented visually
- hypothesizing and predicting
- formulating and asking questions
- understanding and producing technical vocabulary and text features according to content area
- demonstrating knowledge through application in a variety of contexts

Sample Progress Indicators

- identify and associate written symbols with words (e.g., written numerals with spoken numbers, the compass rose with directional words)
- define, compare, and classify objects (e.g., according to number, shape, color, size, function, physical characteristics)
- explain change (e.g., growth in plants and animals, in seasons, in self, in characters in literature)
- record observations
- construct a chart or other graphic showing data
- read a story and represent the sequence of events (through pictures, words, music, or drama)
- locate reference material
- generate and ask questions of outside experts (e.g., about their jobs, experiences, interests, qualifications)
- gather and organize the appropriate materials needed to complete a task
- edit and revise own written assignments
- use contextual clues
- consult print and nonprint resources in the native language when needed

FIGURE 3-2 *(continued)*

PRE-K-3 VIGNETTE

Grade Level:	First grade in a bilingual class
English Proficiency Level:	Mostly beginning, a few intermediate
Language of Instruction:	Spanish and English
Focus of Instruction:	Mathematics
Location:	Suburban school district in the East

Background

The following vignette describes a Spanish/English bilingual first-grade class in a suburban school district. The class consists mostly of immigrant students from the Dominican Republic with a few students of Puerto Rican descent. They are taught by a certified English/Spanish bilingual teacher who is trained to work with ESOL students. Most of the students have a beginning level of proficiency in English, although a few are at a low intermediate level. The students, however, are at different levels of academic (reading and math) readiness. It is early in the school year.

Instructional Sequence

To date, Mr. Quintana has practiced counting with the class as a daily routine, referring to simplified number lines on the desks that the students follow using their fingers. This activity has been extended to counting classroom objects such as desks, chairs, students, rulers, pencils, and so on. The class uses the objects for vocabulary development while learning how to count. In order to strengthen the concept and connection of spoken and written numerals, the results of this daily counting routine have been transcribed often, by using tally marks or numerals on the blackboard, as well as using unifix cubes to represent the objects being counted visually. Several storybooks in English and in Spanish (such as *The Grouchy Ladybug* and *La Oruga Muy Hambrienta*) have been read and reread to the class to introduce counting and measurement with a literature connection.

Today, the class began with a classification activity to introduce the concept of measurement. Students were shown several unifix towers of varying height. The teacher then demonstrated how to organize a sample group from smallest to tallest. Using questions to guide the children, the teacher allowed the students to direct him verbally while arranging the unifix towers according to size. This activity was modeled two more times with individual students acting as teacher while the class provided direction. Then Mr. Quintana used a whole-body activity in which students of varying heights stood in front of class. Through large-group discussion, questions such as: "Who is the smallest?" "Where should he/she stand?" "Who is taller, Mario or Yaritza?" "Where should they stand?" were asked.

Next, the students revisited the activity with the unifix cubes. This time each individual student was given a worksheet that showed several uncolored unifix towers of the exact scale of the actual unifix cubes. The students were then instructed to find the smallest lower on the paper, count, and write the number of cubes underneath. They then verified that it corresponded to the smallest tower that the teacher placed on a

FIGURE 3-2 *(continued)*

table in front of the class. One student volunteered to count the actual tower's cubes so the students could check their work. The students then found the corresponding color among their crayons and colored in the tower. The class continued in this way until each tower was counted and colored.

Then the students cut out the towers to use as manipulatives in classification exercises at their seats as the teacher circulated among students to check for understanding. Next, Mr. Quintana paired the students. Using the student-made unifix paper towers, one student acted as the teacher and placed three or four towers of varying heights in front of the partner. The other student arranged his or her objects accordingly.

For homework, students were asked to draw pictures of their family members according to height, from tallest to shortest.

Discussion

Students are encouraged to
- identify and associate written symbols with words (e.g., written numerals with spoken numbers, the compass rose with directional words)
- define, compare, and classify objects (e.g., according to number, shape, color, size, function, physical characteristics)
- record observations

Mr. Quintana's bilingual first-grade class is composed of nonnative speakers of English. In this vignette the students are using English to reinforce counting and to explore the concept of measurement and classification in their math class. All the students know how to count in Spanish. Here, in this instructional sequence, the students are given the opportunity to learn and practice academic English through verbal communication. The National Council of Teachers of Mathematics (1989) *Curriculum and Evaluation Standards for School Mathematics* suggest that "it is important, therefore, to provide opportunities for [the students] to 'talk mathematics.' Interacting with classmates helps children construct knowledge, learn other ways to think about ideas, and clarify their own thinking" (p. 26). This instructional sequence provides these opportunities to "talk math" in large-group and small-group activities.

The routines in Mr. Quintana's class reveal a twofold purpose: first, the routines allow beginning-level students to increase their oral comprehension through the use of formulaic phrases; second, the routines build a foundational knowledge of mathematics upon which more complex concepts can be built. This is a helpful process for students who are learning English. Mr. Quintana's careful connection of the spoken and written word, as well as his use of the different systems for writing numbers (e.g., tally marks, numerals) is also important for the bilingual students. Moreover, by using concrete objects the students are familiar with, combined with highly predictable, formulaic utterances, he helps the students recognize the role mathematics has in their lives.

Mr. Quintana allows the students to explore concrete objects and math manipulatives in order to learn basic math concepts. The students begin with a hands-on activity to count and organize cubes in unifix towers. They then proceed to two-dimensional representations of the

FIGURE 3-2 *(continued)*

manipulatives. This vital step helps the students make the connection between the objects that they handled and the objects that they will see on paper in future assignments. At this point they make observations about the number of cubes in the towers and record them. These observations are then checked against the three-dimensional models. Mr. Quintana also teaches them comparative language forms, such as taller, smallest, and so forth.

The home-school connection is strengthened through a follow-up activity in which the heights of family members are compared with each other. Students at all levels of proficiency can draw representations of family members and classify them by size.

Source: Teachers of English to Speakers of Other Languages, Inc. *ESL Standards for Pre-K-12 Students*, pp. 49-52. Alexandria, VA: Teachers of English to Speakers of Other Languages, Inc. Copyright 1997 by Teachers of English to Speakers of Other Languages, Inc. Reprinted with permission. For more information, or to obtain a coy of the full *Standards* volume, please contact TESOL's publication assistant: Tel. 703-836-0074; Fax 703-836-7864; E-mail publ@tesol.edu; http://www.tesol.edu/.

CHAPTER 4

Assessments of Student Performance

STANDARDS-BASED ASSESSMENT

Assessments have long held a strong influence on educational practice, particularly in Title I. From its inception, Title I required the use of "appropriate objective measures of educational achievement" in order to ensure that the program was achieving its goal of reducing the achievement gap between low-income and higher-income students. In carrying out this requirement, states and school districts, for the most part, used standardized norm-referenced tests to measure the achievement of eligible students—both to determine eligibility and to measure gains. As a result, Title I increased dramatically the number of tests states and districts administered; one district administrator estimated that the Title I requirements doubled the amount of testing in the district (Office of Technology Assessment, 1992).

The influence of the federal program on schools was not always healthy, and many critics argued that the tests actually contributed to the limited improvement in student performance the program demonstrated (Advisory Committee on Testing in Chapter 1, 1993). In particular, some critics charged that the tests contributed to undesirable instructional practices. Because of the great weight attached to test scores, the critics contended, teachers tended to overemphasize test-taking strategies or the relatively low-level skills the tests measured, rather than focus on more challenging abilities or demanding content. At the same time, critics pointed out, many schools placed less emphasis than they might have placed on topics or subjects not tested, such as science and social studies.

In addition, critics noted that the tests failed to provide timely or useful information for teachers; that states and districts inappropriately used the tests as exclusive instruments to determine educational need; and that the aggregate data accumulated from the various districts and states were incomplete and of mixed quality.

The 1994 reauthorization of Title I was intended to change all that. The goal of the law was to harness the power of assessment to positive ends, using assessments to drive challenging instruction for all students. The mechanism for doing so was the requirement that assessments be "aligned" to the challenging standards for student performance. Teaching students to do well on the tests would mean that students would be learning what they needed to achieve the standards. Moreover, the assessment data would inform students, parents, teachers, and members of the public how well students were performing against the standards, rather than in comparison to other students.

In its effort to use assessment to promote instructional change, the Title I law was also tapping in to a reform movement in assessment. Like the critics of Title I testing, assessment critics contended that the traditional tests used in most schools and school districts—typically, norm-referenced, multiple-choice tests—narrowed the curriculum to the low-level knowledge and skills tested and provided inadequate and sometimes misleading information about student performance. In part, these critics drew on data showing the effects of the tests on instruction. But they also drew on a strain of research on student learning that emphasized the importance of students' abilities to use their knowledge to solve problems that reflect the world they encounter outside the classroom. To assess such abilities—and to promote instruction that fosters the development of such abilities in children—reformers called for new assessments that would measure student abilities to understand, analyze, and organize knowledge to solve complex problems.

These assessments, for example, might ask students to gather data and determine the mathematical procedures necessary to design a solution involving architecture or flying. Or they might ask students to read historical documents and analyze what they've read, together with what they know from other sources, to interpret a key event in history. Or they might ask students to conduct a science experiment in order to come up with a reasoned argument on an environmental issue.

In addition to tapping student knowledge in new ways, these types of assessments are also aimed at reporting results differently from traditional tests. Most significantly, the results would indicate whether students had attained challenging standards that demanded that they demonstrate such abilities.

indings

Alignment. The ability of tests to reach all the ambitious goals set out by reformers depends, first of all, on the *alignment* between tests and standards. Alignment is a necessary condition of the theory of action of standards-based reform; indeed, the Title I statute requires state assessments to "be aligned with the State's challenging content and performance standards." Alignment ensures that the tests match the learning goals embodied in the standards. At the same time, aligned assessments enable the public to determine student progress toward the standards.

A study conducted for the committee found that alignment may be difficult to achieve (Wixson et al., 1999). The study examined assessments and standards in elementary reading in four states. Using a method developed by Webb (1997), the researchers analyzed the cognitive complexity of both the standards and the assessment items, and estimated the extent to which the assessment actually measured the standards.

The study found that, of the four states, two had a high degree of alignment, one was poorly aligned, and one was moderately aligned. Of the two highly aligned states, one, State A, achieved its alignment, at least in part, because it relied on the commercial norm-referenced test it used to develop its standards, and the standards were the least cognitively complex of any of the states analyzed. State B, whose standards were at the highest level of cognitive complexity, meanwhile, had the lowest degree of alignment; only 30 percent of its objectives were measured by the state-developed test.

The other two states administered two tests to measure reading. In State C, which had a high degree of alignment, the state-developed comprehension test measured essentially the same content and cognitive levels as the norm-referenced test. In State D, however, a second test—an oral-reading test—did make a difference in alignment. But overall, that state's assessments and standards were moderately aligned.

The Wixson study suggests a number of possible reasons why attaining alignment is difficult. One has to do with the way states went about building their assessments. Unless a state deliberately designed a test to measure its standards—or developed standards to match the test, as State A did in the study—it is unlikely that the test and the standards will be aligned, particularly if a state uses an off-the-shelf test. Commercial tests designed for off-the-shelf use are deliberately designed to sell in many states; since standards vary widely from state to state, such tests are unlikely to line up with any single state's standards. Thus states using commercial tests are likely to find gaps between the tests and their standards.

But even when states set out to develop a test to measure their standards, they are likely to find gaps as well. In large part, this is because a single test is unlikely to tap all of a state's standards, particularly the extensive lists of standards some states have adopted. In addition, the ability of tests to tap standards may be limited by the constraints imposed on tests, such as testing time and cost. Time constraints have forced some states to limit tests to a few hours in length, and as a result, they can seldom include enough items to measure every standard sufficiently. Financial constraints, meanwhile, have led states to rely more heavily on machine-scored items, rather than items that are scored by hand. And at this point, many performance-based tasks—which measure standards such as writing skill and the ability to communicate mathematically—require more costly hand scoring.

Similarly, the technical requirements for tests—particularly when consequences are attached to the results—have led some states to limit the use of performance items. Researchers have found that the technical quality of some performance items may have been insufficiently strong for use in high-stakes situations (Western Michigan University Evaluation Center, 1995; Koretz et al., 1993; Cronbach et al., 1994).

Researchers at the National Center for Research on Evaluation, Standards, and Student Testing (CRESST) have developed an approach to building performance assessment that is designed to link directly the expectations for learning embedded in content standards to the tasks on the assessment. Known as model-based performance assessment, the approach combines a means of enabling states and districts to assess student learning against standards with a way, through clear specifications, of providing instructional guidance to classroom teachers (Baker et al., 1991, 1999; Baker, 1997; Glaser, 1991; Mislevy, 1993; Niemi, 1997; Webb and Romberg, 1992).

Validity of Inferences. The ability of tests to accomplish the reformers' aims of reporting student progress on standards and informing instruction depends on the validity of the inferences one can draw from the assessment information. For individual students, a one- or two-hour test can provide only a small amount of information about knowledge and skill in a domain; a test composed of performance items can provide even less information (although the quality of the information is quite different). For classrooms, schools, and school districts, the amount of information such tests can provide is greater, since the limited information from individual students can be aggregated and random errors of measurement will cancel each other out.

Yet the information available from large-scale tests about the performance of schools and school districts is still limited. One reason for this is because overall averages mask the performance of groups within the total, and the averages may be misleading. This is particularly problematic because variations within schools tend to be greater than variations among schools (Willms, 1998). For example, consider two schools. School A has a high proportion of high-achieving students, yet its low-achieving students perform very poorly. School B has fewer high performers than School A, yet its lower-achieving students perform considerably better than those at School A do. Using only average scores, a district policy maker might conclude that School A is more effective than School B, even though a number of students in School A perform at low levels. School B's success in raising the performance of its lower-achieving students, meanwhile, would get lost.

Determining whether a school's superior performance is the result of superior instructional practices is difficult in any case, because academic performance depends on many factors, only some of which the school can control (Raudenbush and Willms, 1995). Because of differences in student composition, test scores by themselves say little about "school effects," or the influence of attending a particular school on student performance. However, using statistical techniques to control for student background factors, Raudenbush and Willms (1995) have shown that it is possible to compute at least the upper and lower bounds of school effects. Separately, Sanders (Sanders and Horn, 1995) has developed a statistical method to calculate the effect on student performance of individual teachers within a school. Sanders's method has been used in several districts to determine the "value added" that teachers provide.

Instructional Sensitivity. Tests vary in the extent to which they respond to and inform instructional practice. Many tests, particularly those designed to test a range of standards, are relatively insensitive to instruction; changing teaching practices to reflect standards may not result in higher test scores on such assessments. But even tests that do capture the results of instructional improvement may not be as informative as they might; the ways the tests are scaled and results are reported tell little about what caused students to succeed or not succeed.

Determining the instructional sensitivity of assessments requires careful study of classroom practices and their relations to student performance. To carry out such studies, researchers need data on the type of instruction students receive. By showing whether instructional practices related to the standards produce gains in assessment performance while other practices do not, researchers can demonstrate whether an assessment is instructionally sensitive (Cohen and Hill, 1998; Yoon and Resnick, 1998).

Multiple Purposes. Tests should be constructed in different ways, depending on the purpose for which they are used. A test intended to inform the public and policy makers about the condition of education is more likely than other types of tests to include a broad range of items designed to provide information about students' mastery of, say, 8th grade mathematics. These tests are typically administered at most once a year, and often the results come back too late for teachers to use them to make adjustments in their instructional programs.

A test intended for instructional guidance, in contrast, is more likely than others to include items that tap a particular topic—say, algebra—in greater depth, so that teachers have an idea of students' specific knowledge and skills, and possible misconceptions. These tests, usually administered by classroom teachers, are given relatively frequently.

The technical quality of a test should be appropriate for its intended use. For measures used for accountability, system monitoring, and program evaluation, the Standards for Educational and Psychological Testing (American Educational Research Association, American Psychological Association, National Council on Measurement in Education, 1985; in press) should be followed. These standards include guidelines for validity, reliability, fairness, test development, and protection of test takers' rights.

Using the same test for multiple purposes poses problems. The broad, public-information-type of test will provide too little information too infrequently to help teachers redesign their instructional practices to address the particular needs of their students. The instructional-guidance test will provide too little information about the range of student knowledge and skills in a subject area—or may be misinterpreted to suggest more than it actually offers. At the same time, instructional guidance tests are often scored by teachers; using such tests for accountability purposes may provide an incentive for teachers to report the best possible results, throwing into question the accuracy and value of the information they provide.

Yet undue attention on the accountability measure encourages schools to focus all their efforts on raising the performance on that measure, which may not be equivalent to improving performance generally. In some cases, schools resort to inappropriate practices, such as teaching specific test items, or items like test items, in order to raise scores. These practices do little to improve student learning (Shepard, 1989; Koretz et al., 1991).

However, preliminary evidence suggests that careful attention to instructional guidance assessments appears to contribute to higher performance. Principals who testified before the committee described the way their schools used regular and frequent teacher-made assessments to monitor the progress of every student and to gauge the effectiveness of the instructional program. And a study of successful high-poverty schools in Texas found that such schools administered frequent assessments and used the data in their instructional planning (Ragland et al., 1999). These schools used assessment data from classroom assessments, district tests, and state tests to develop a well-rounded picture of student performance in order to make decisions about instructional strategies.

ecommendations

• Teachers should administer assessments frequently and regularly in classrooms for the purpose of monitoring individual students' performance and adapting instruction to improve their performance.

• Assessment should involve a range of strategies appropriate for inferences relevant to individual students, classrooms, schools, districts, and states.

• The overwhelming majority of standards-based assessments should be sensitive to effective instruction—that is, they should detect the effects of high-quality teaching. Districts, schools, and teachers should use the results of these assessments to revise their practices to help students improve performance.

• Standardized, norm-referenced tests of content knowledge should be used as indicators of performance and should not be the focus of instruction.

• Multiple measures should be combined in such a way that enables individuals and schools to demonstrate competency in a variety of ways. Such measures should work together to support the coherence of instruction.

uestions to Ask

❑ Do schools conduct regular assessments of individual students' performance and use the data to adjust their instructional programs?

❑ Do assessments include a range of strategies appropriate for their purposes?

❑ Do the state, district, and schools collect information to determine the instructional sensitivity of their assessments?

❑ Do multiple measures, including district and state tests, complement one another and enable schools to develop a coherent instructional program?

riteria

As states and districts develop assessments, the committee recommends using the following criteria:

Coherence. Assessments are most efficient and effective when various measures complement each other. Assessments should be designed to measure different standards, or to provide different types of information to different constituents. In designing assessments, states or districts should examine the assessments already in place at various levels and determine the needs to be filled.

Transparency. Results from the array of assessments should be reported so that students, teachers, parents, and the general public understand how they were derived and what they mean.

Validity. The inferences from tests are valid when the information from the test can support them. Validity depends on the way a test is used. Inferences that may be valid for one purpose—for example, determining eligibility for a particular program—may not be supportable for another—such as program evaluation. Validity of inferences depends on technical quality; the stability and consistency of the measurement help determine whether the inferences drawn from it can be supported.

Fairness. A test must produce appropriate inferences for all students; results should not be systematically inaccurate for any identifiable subgroup. In addition, results should not be reported in ways that are unfair to any group of students.

Credibility. Tests and test results must be believable to the constituents of test information. A test that supports valid inferences, that is fair, and that is instructionally sensitive may not provide meaningful information or foster changes in practice if teachers or policy makers do not trust the information they receive from the test.

Utility. Tests will serve their purpose only if users understand the results and can act on them. To this end, tests must be clear in describing student achievement, in suggesting areas for improvement of practice, in determining the progress of schools and school districts, and in informing parents and policy makers about the state of student and school performance.

Practicality. Faced with constraints on time and cost, states and districts should focus their assessment on the highest-priority standards. They should examine existing measures at the state and district levels and implement assessments that complement measures already in place.

 xamples

The following two examples of assessments come from districts pursuing standards-based reform. Each district has created a mosaic of assessment information that includes frequent assessments of individual student progress at the classroom level; portfolios and grade conferences on student work at the school level; performance assessments at the district level; and standards-referenced tests at the state level. All of these are compiled into reports that show important constituencies what they need to know about student performance.

> Community District 2 in New York City began its reform effort by changing the curriculum, rather than the assessments. The district administers a citywide mathematics and reading test, and a state test as well. Each year, the district reviews the results, school by school, with principals and the board, setting specific goals for raising performance, especially among the lowest-performing students. In addition, schools also administer additional assessments that they found are aligned with the curriculum. In that way, the intensive staff development around curriculum, which the district has made its hallmark, and the professional development the district provided on the assessment, produce the same result: teachers with significantly enhanced knowledge and skills about how to teach students toward challenging standards.

Schools in Boston also use a multifaceted approach to assessment. The state of Massachusetts has developed its own test, and the district uses a commercial test. In addition, schools have developed parallel assessments. One elementary school, for example, begins each September by assessing every student, from early childhood to grade 5, using a variety of methods: observation for young children (through grade 2), running records, writing samples. They repeat the running records and writing samples every four to six weeks. They examine the data in January and again in June to determine the children's progress. In that way, every teacher can tell you how her students are doing at any point. Teachers can adjust their instructional practices accordingly, and principals have a clear picture of how each classroom is performing. The district and state tests, meanwhile, provide an estimate of each school's performance for policy makers.

ASSESSING YOUNG CHILDREN

The 1994 Title I statute poses a problem for educators and policy makers interested in determining the progress of large numbers of disadvantaged students. Although 49 percent of children served by the program are in grades 3 and below, the law does not require states to establish assessments before grade 3. Without some form of assessment, schools and districts would have no way of determining the progress of this large group of students.

The law's emphasis on testing in grade 3 and above followed practice in the states, many of which have in recent years reduced their use of tests in the early grades. Only 5 states test students in grade 2; 3 test in grade 1; and 2 test in kindergarten (Council of Chief State School Officers, 1998).

The federal and state actions reflect their responses to the arguments of early childhood educators. These educators have long been committed to the ongoing assessment of young children for the purpose of instructional improvement. Indeed, ongoing assessment of children in their natural settings is part and parcel of high-quality early childhood educators' training. However, early childhood educators have raised serious questions about the use of tests for accountability purposes in the early grades, particularly tests used for making decisions about student tracking and promotion.

The press for accountability in education generally, along with the increasing emphasis on the early years, has brought the issue of early childhood assessment to the fore. Among state and district policy makers, the question of how best to assess and test young children, and how to do so in ways that are appropriate and productive, remains an issue of great concern and debate.

Findings

Assessing the knowledge and skills of children younger than age 8 poses many of the same problems as assessments of older children, as well as posing some unique problems. Like tests for older children, tests for young children should be appropriate to the purpose for which they are used, and they must support whatever inferences are drawn from the results.

The National Education Goals Panel's Goal 1 Early Childhood Assessment Resource Group (Shepard et al., 1998a) identified four purposes for assessment of children before age 8, each of which demands its own method and instrumentation. The four purposes are:

Instructional Improvement. Measures aimed at supporting teaching and learning are designed to inform students, parents, and teachers about student progress and development and to identify areas in which further instruction is needed. Such measures may include direct observations of children during classroom activities; evaluation of samples of work; asking questions orally; and asking informed adults about the child.

Identification for Special Needs. Measures aimed at identifying special problems inform parents, teachers, and specialists about the possible existence of physical or learning disabilities that may require services beyond those provided in a regular classroom.

Program Evaluation. Measures aimed at evaluating programs inform parents, policy makers, and the public about trends in student performance and the effectiveness of educational programs.

Accountability. Measures to hold individuals, teachers, or schools accountable for performance inform parents, policy makers, and the public about the extent to which students and schools are meeting external standards for performance.

In practice, however, tests for young children have been used for purposes for which they were not intended, and, as a result, inferences about children's abilities or the quality of early childhood education programs have been erroneous, sometimes with harmful effects (Shepard, 1994). For example, schools have used test results to retain children in grade, despite evidence that retention does not improve academic performance and could increase the likelihood that children will drop out of school. In addition, schools have also used tests to put students into academic tracks prematurely and inappropriately (National Research Council, 1999a).

These problems have been exacerbated by the type of assessments typically used for accountability purposes—group-administered paper-and-pencil tests—which may be inappropriate for young children (Graue, 1999, Meisels, 1996). Such tests often fail to capture children's learning over time or predict their growth trajectory with accuracy, and they often reflect an outmoded view of learning. In contrast to older children, young children tend to learn in episodic and idiosyncratic ways; a task that frustrates a child on Tuesday may be easily accomplished a week later. In addition, children younger than 8 have little experience taking tests and may not be able to demonstrate their knowledge and skills well on such instruments. A paper-and-pencil test may not provide an accurate representation of what a young child knows and can do.

However, the types of assessments useful for instructional improvement, identification of special needs, and program evaluation may not be appropriate for use in providing accountability data. Instructional improvement and identification rely on measures such as direct observations of student activities or portfolios of student work, which raise issues of reliability and validity if used for accountability (Graue, 1999). Program evaluations include a wide range of measures—including measures of student physical well-being and motor skills, social development, and approaches to learning, as well as cognitive and language development—which may be prohibitively expensive to collect for all students.

However, it is possible to obtain large-scale information about what students have learned and what teachers have taught by using instructional assessments. By aggregating this information, district and state policy makers can use data on instructional assessment to chart the progress of children in the first years of schooling without encountering the problems associated with early childhood assessment noted above. To ensure accuracy, a state or district can "audit" the results of these assessments by having highly trained educators independently verify a representative sample of teacher-scored assessments. Researchers at the Educational Testing Service have found that such an approach can produce valid and reliable information about literacy performance (Bridgeman et al., 1995).

A second strategy might be to assess the full range of abilities that young children are expected to develop, and hold schools accountable for their progress in enabling children to develop such abilities, by assessing representative samples of young children. To ensure the validity of inferences from such assessments, the samples should represent all students in a school; sample sizes can be sufficiently large to indicate the performance of groups of children, particularly the disadvantaged students who are the intended beneficiaries of Title I. Individual scores would not be reported. Researchers are exploring methodologies to describe levels or patterns of growth, ability, or developmental levels.

monitor the progress of individual children in
prove the quality and appropriateness of
ments should be conducted at multiple
n's natural settings, and should use direct
hecklists, and other work sampling devices.
measure all domains of children's develop-
evelopment, reading, and mathematics.
countable for promoting high levels of
performance for primary grade students.
in grades 1 and 2, states and districts
ty through the use of representative
ssessment of every pupil.
s, foundations, and other funding agen-
rch that advances knowledge of how to
mathematics performance for both instruc-
y purposes.

Questions ... sk

❑ Do teachers regularly asse.. the progress of students in early grades for the purpose of instructional improvement?

❑ Is there in place a comprehensive assessment to hold schools accountable for the performance of children before grade 3? Does the assessment include measures of children's physical well-being and motor skills, approaches to learning, and language and cognitive development?

❑ Does the assessment in the early grades measure performance of a representative sample of students? Or is an "audit" used to monitor a sample of teacher-administered and teacher-scored assessments?

Criteria

Assessments for young children should follow the same criteria used for assessments generally, which were described above. In addition, such assessments should also meet additional criteria based on the unique problems associated with testing children from birth to age 8. The committee recommends that, in developing an assessment system for young children, states and districts should adhere to the following criteria:

Appropriateness. Assessments should reflect the un[...] needs and characteristics of young children, and should b[...] purposes for which they are intended. Information shou[...] multiple points in time in settings that are not threateni[...]

Coherence. The assessment of young children sho[...] districts with information about student performance[...] instructional goals for older students.

xamples

The following examples describe two approac[...] mance of young children that provide information[...] in early grades toward standards with methods that[...] yield valid and reliable information. The assessm[...] tional improvement by providing teachers with i[...] students' performance. The South Brunswick asse[...] districts and states should supplement such an asses[...] physical and motor development.

> The South Brunswick, New Jersey Public Schoo[...] and implemented an early literacy portfolio asses[...]nts in grades K-2. Under the system, students collect v[...] in a portfolio that they carry with them all three years. Teac[...] rate the work on a 1-to-6 developmental scale; the ratings [...] moderated by ratings by another teacher. The ratings are aggregated by school and reported to the district. The district's goal is for all students to be at the 5.5-6 level by the end of 2nd grade.
>
> The portfolio system was developed to follow two key principles. First, teachers believe that no high-stakes decision about a child or a teacher should be based on a single form of evidence. They therefore designed the system so that it includes various forms of assessment, such as observations of children's activities, work samples, and "test-like activities"—that is, on-demand responses to prompts. Second, they believe that the assessment should serve both a means of professional development and as an accountability measure. This system accomplishes this dual goal by allowing teachers to see information about student performance as work in a portfolio, not as points on a scale, and thus understand how to teach their own students, and by allowing the district to monitor school performance through the aggregated scores.
>
> The Work Sampling System, which is in use in a number of districts, is an authentic, curriculum-embedded performance assessment. Developed at the University of Michigan, the assessment is based on teachers' observations of children at work in the class-

room—learning, solving problems, interacting with others, and creating products. Designed for students in preschool through grade 5, the Work Sampling System consists of three interrelated elements: developmental guidelines and checklists, portfolios, and summary reports. A brief observational assessment version of Work Sampling designed for Title I reporting is also available.

Studies of Work Sampling's effectiveness in urban communities, and particularly in Title I settings, demonstrate that the assessment is an accurate measure of children's progress and performance. It is a low-stakes, nonstigmatizing assessment that relies on extensive sampling of children's academic, personal, and social progress over the school year and provides a rich source of information about student strengths and weaknesses. In professional development associated with the system, teachers learn to observe, document, and evaluate student performance during actual classroom lessons. Through the checklists and other materials, teachers can translate their students' work into the data of assessment by systematically documenting and evaluating it, using specific criteria and well-defined procedures (Meisels, 1996).

ASSESSING STUDENTS WITH DISABILITIES

One of the most far-reaching features of the 1994 Title I statute was its requirement to include all students in assessment and accountability mechanisms, and in its definition of "all students," the law refers specifically to students with disabilities. According to the law, states must "provide for the participation of all students in the grades being assessed." To accomplish this, the law calls for "reasonable adaptations and accommodations" for students with diverse learning needs.

This requirement was reinforced and strengthened by the Individuals with Disabilities Education Act of 1997. That law requires states to demonstrate that children with disabilities are included in general state and district-wide assessment programs, with appropriate accommodations and modifications, if necessary. The law further states that the individualized education program (IEP), which is required to be developed for each student with a disability, must indicate the modifications required for the child to take part in the assessment; if the IEP process determines that a student is unable to participate in any part of an assessment program, the IEP must demonstrate why the student cannot participate and how the student will be assessed.

The law also requires states to develop alternate assessments for children who cannot participate in state and district-wide assessments, and to report to the public on the number of students with disabilities participating in regular and alternate assessment programs, and the performance of such students on the assessments.

These provisions break new ground. In the past, as many as half of all students with disabilities have not taken part in state and district-wide assessments (National Research Council, 1999a). Although state policies vary widely, one survey found that 37 states in 1998 allowed exemptions from all assessments for students with disabilities, and another 10 allowed exemptions from some assessments for such students (Council of Chief State School Officers, 1998).

In addition, although many states have allowed students with disabilities to take the tests with accommodations and adaptations, the policies that determine which students qualify for accommodations have varied, and test results for students who are administered accommodated assessments have often been excluded from school reports.

Excluding such students from assessments and accountability is problematic. First, it sends a signal that such students do not matter, or that educators have low expectations for them, and that states and districts are not responsible for their academic progress. Second, exclusion throws into question the validity of school and district reports on performance; if such reports do not include the performance of a significant number of students, do they truly represent the level of student performance in a school or district? Third, leaving students with disabilities out of assessments deprives such students, their parents, and their teachers of the benefits of information on their progress toward standards.

Yet while including all students in assessments may be a worthwhile goal, doing so poses enormous problems. While for some students with disabilities, state and district tests yield valid and reliable information, for many others, the effects of accommodations on the meaning and validity of test results is unknown.

indings

The population of students with disabilities is diverse. Altogether, about 10 percent of the school population is identified as having a disability. Such disabilities range from mild to severe, and include physical, sensory, behavioral, and cognitive impairments. Some 90 percent of the students who qualify for special services under the Individuals with Disabilities Education Act (IDEA) fall in the categories of either the speech or language impairment, serious emotional disturbance, mental retardation, or specific learning disability; of these, half have learning disabilities. However, the definitions of those categories vary from school district to school district and from state to state. Some have argued that the decision to classify students as having a disability may have more to do with educational policy and practices than with the students' physical or mental capabilities (National Research Council, 1997a).

Students who qualify for special education services under the IDEA are educated according to the terms of an individual education program (IEP), which is a program negotiated by the child's parents, the school, and service providers. Although evidence varies on the effectiveness of such plans, particularly the degree to which they provide accountability, the IEP has become paramount in determining the services children with disabilities receive (Smith, 1990). Among other provisions, the IEP has generally determined whether or not a student will participate in testing programs, and if so, under what circumstances.

Participation in testing programs has varied. In addition to the number of students who have been excluded from tests, many others have taken tests that accommodate them in some way. States and districts generally employ four types of accommodations to tests (Thurlow et al., 1997):

- presentation format, or changes in ways tests were presented, such as Braille versions or oral reading;
- response format, or changes in the way students could give their responses, such as allowing them to point or use a computer;
- setting of the test, or changes in the place or situation in which a student takes a test, such as allowing students to take the test at home or in a small group; and
- timing, or changes in the length or structure of a test, such as allowing extended time or frequent breaks.

As the National Research Council's Committee on Goals 2000 and the Inclusion of Students With Disabilities found, the number of students who need such accommodations is unknown. Moreover, the extent to which states and districts employ any or all of these accommodations varies widely, depending on the population of the state, the state's standards and assessments, and other factors (National Research Council, 1997a).

However, because most students with disabilities have only mild impairments, the vast majority can participate in assessments with accommodations. Only a small number of the most cognitively disabled students, whose educational goals differ from the regular curriculum, will be required to take alternate assessments under the IDEA.

Despite the common use of such accommodations, however, there is little research on their effects on the validity of test score information, and most of the research has examined college admission tests and other postsecondary measures, not achievement tests in elementary and secondary schools (National Research Council, 1997a).

Because of the paucity of research, questions remain about whether test results from assessments using accommodations represent valid and reliable indicators of what students with disabilities know and are able to do (Koretz, 1997). But a number of studies are under way to determine appropriate methods of including students with disabilities in assessments, including the National Assessment of Educational Progress (National Research Council, 1999a).

Recommendations

- Assessments should be administered regularly and frequently for the purpose of monitoring the progress of individual students with disabilities and for adapting instruction to improve performance.
- States and districts should develop clear guidelines for accommodations that permit students with disabilities to participate in assessments administered for accountability purposes.
- States and districts should collect evidence to demonstrate that the assessment, with accommodations, can measure the knowledge or skill of particular students or groups of students.
- States and districts should describe the methods they use to screen students for accommodations, and they should report the frequency of these practices.
- Federal research units, foundations, and other funding agencies should promote research that advances knowledge about the validity and reliability of different accommodations and alternate assessment practices.

Questions to Ask

❏ Are clear guidelines in place for accommodations that permit students with disabilities to participate in assessments administered for accountability purposes?

❏ Is there evidence that the assessment, with accommodations, can measure the knowledge or skill of particular students or groups of students?

❏ Are the methods used to screen students to determine whether they need accommodations for tests reported, including the frequency of such practices?

Criteria

Assessments for students with disabilities should follow the same criteria used for assessments generally, which were described above. In addition, such assessments should also meet additional criteria based on the unique problems associated with testing children with disabilities. The committee recommends that, in developing an assessment system for students with disabilities, states and districts adhere to the following criteria:

Inclusion. The assessments should provide a means of including all students; alternate assessments should be used only when students are so cognitively impaired that their curriculum is qualitatively different from that of students in the regular education program. The state or district should provide accommodations for those who can participate in the regular assessment.

Appropriateness. States and districts need to ensure that accommodations meet the needs of students, and that tests administered under different conditions represent accurate measures of students' knowledge and skills.

Documentation. States and districts should develop and document policies regarding the basis for assigning accommodations to students and for reporting the results of students who have taken tests with accommodations.

Examples

The following two examples describe state policies for assessing students with disabilities. Each sets as a goal including such students in the assessments, and each specifies the criteria for the use of accommodations. State policies should also call for documentation of the use of accommodations and for reporting results for students administered accommodated assessments.

> According to Maryland state policy, "all students have a legal right to be included to the fullest extent possible in all statewide assessment programs and to have their assessment results be a part of Maryland's accountability system." To accomplish this goal, the state department of education has developed guidelines for when students should receive accommodations, which accommodations are permissible for which tests, and when students may be excused or exempted from the tests.
>
> Under the policy, accommodations:
>
> - Enable students to participate more fully in assessments and to better demonstrate their knowledge and skills;
> - Must be based on individual students' needs and not a category of disability, level of intensity, level of instruction, time spent in mainstream classroom, or program setting;
> - Must be justified and documented in the individualized education program (IEP);
> - Must not invalidate the assessment for which they are granted.
>
> Students may be excused from assessments if they demonstrate "inordinate frustration, distress or disruption of others." Decisions to exempt students must be made during an IEP committee meeting. Students who are not pursuing Maryland Learning Outcomes may be exempted.
>
> Excused students are counted in the denominator for determining

the school's scores on the Maryland Student Performance Assessment Program.

Permitted accommodations include: scheduling accommodations, such as periodic breaks; setting accommodations, such as special seating or seating in small groups; equipment/technology accommodations, such as large print, Braille, or mechanical spellers or other electronic devices; presentation accommodations, such as repetition of directions, sign-language interpreters, or access to close-caption or video materials; and response accommodations, such as pointing, student tape responses, or dictation. If an accommodation alters the skill being tested—such as allowing a student to dictate answers on a writing test—the student will not receive a score on that portion of the test.

In Alabama, where the state requires students to pass an exit examination in order to earn a regular high school diploma, the state has developed guidelines to enable all students—including students with disabilities—to take the exam and earn the diploma. Under the guidelines, if an IEP team determines from test data, teacher evaluations, and other sources that the student will work toward the Alabama high school diploma, the student must receive instruction in the content on the exit examination. The IEP team also determines the accommodations the student will require in order to take the exam.

The state permits accommodations in scheduling, setting, format and equipment, and recording. The guidelines note that "an accommodation cannot be provided if it changes the nature, content, or integrity of the test. In addition, they state that students of special populations must be given practice in taking tests similar in content and format to those of the state test prior to participating in an assessment.

In all, more than 2,100 tenth graders in special education took the pregraduation examination in 1999, about 5 percent of the total who took the test that year.

ASSESSING ENGLISH LANGUAGE LEARNERS

The requirement in the 1994 Title I statute to include "all students" in assessments and accountability provisions also refers to students for whom English is a second language. In order to "provide for the participation of all students in the grades being assessed," the law called for states to assess English language learners "to the extent practicable, in the language and form most likely to yield accurate and reliable information on what these students know and can do to determine the students' mastery of skills in subjects other than English."

As with students with disabilities, this provision represents a substantial departure from conventional practice for English-language learners. According to the 1998 survey by the Council of Chief State School Officers, 29 states allow exemptions from all testing requirements for English-language learners, while another 11 states allow exemptions from some assessments for such students (Council of Chief State School Officers, 1998). In addition, all but 7 states allow some form of accommodation for English-language learners; however, students who are administered accommodated assessments are often excluded from school reports.

Excluding English-language learners from assessments raises the same issues that excluding students with disabilities brings to the fore: excluded students "do not count," the exclusions throw into question the meaning and validity of test score reports, and students, parents, and teachers miss out on the information tests provide. Yet including such students also poses substantial challenges, and doing so inappropriately can produce misleading results. For example, an English-language mathematics test for students not proficient in the language will yield misleading inferences about such students' knowledge and skills in mathematics.

indings

As with students with disabilities, the population of students for whom English is not the primary language is diverse. According to the U.S. Department of Education's Office of Bilingual Education and Language Minority Affairs, there are 3.2 million limited-English-proficient students nationwide in 1998, nearly twice as many as there were a decade before. Nearly three-fourths of the English-language learners speak Spanish, but the population includes students from many other language groups, including Vietnamese (3.9 percent), Hmong (1.8 percent), Cantonese (1.7 percent), and Cambodian (1.6 percent).

In addition to the diversity in native languages, English-language learners also vary in their academic skills. Some students may have come to the United States after years of extensive schooling in their native country, and they may be quite proficient in content areas. Others may have had only sketchy schooling before arriving in this country.

Moreover, those who are learning English do so at different rates, and they may be at different points in their proficiency in the language. For the most part, receptive language—reading and listening—develops before productive language—writing and speaking. As a result, a test given to students who have developed receptive language may underestimate these students' abilities, since they can understand more than they can express.

To help educators determine the level of students' English-language proficiency, the Teachers of English to Students of Other Languages, the Center for Applied Linguistics, and the National Association for Bilingual Education have developed a set of standards (Teachers of English to Speakers of Other Languages, 1997). These standards complement the subject-area standards developed by other national organizations; they acknowledge the central role of language in the learning of content as well as the particular instructional needs of learners who are in the process of developing proficiency in English.

States have attempted to deal with the variability in students' English proficiency by developing policies to exempt students with limited English proficiency from statewide tests. But the criteria vary among the states. In most cases, the time the student has spent in the United States is the determining factor; in others, the time the student has spent in an English-as-a-second-language program has governed such decisions. However, some have argued that time is not the critical factor and instead have recommended that students demonstrate language proficiency before states and districts determine whether they will participate in assessments. A few states use such determinations, formally or informally (Council of Chief State School Officers, 1998).

In addition to exempting English-language learners from tests, most states permit some form of accommodations for such students. The most common accommodations are in presentation, such as repeating directions, having a familiar person administer the test, and reading directions orally; in timing, such as extending the length of the testing period and permitting breaks; and in setting, such as administering tests in small groups or in separate rooms. A few states also permit modifications in response format, such as permitting students to respond in their native language.

In addition to the modifications, 11 states also have in place alternate assessments for English-language learners. Most commonly these alternatives take the form of foreign-language versions of the test. In most cases, these versions are in Spanish; New York State provides tests in Russian, Chinese, Korean, and Haitian Creole as well. The second-language versions are not simple translations, however. Translations would not capture idioms or other features unique to a language or culture.

Second-language assessments are controversial. Since the purpose of the test is to measure students' knowledge and skills in content areas, many states have provided alternate assessments in subjects other than English; to test English ability, states have continued to rely on English-language assessments. The voluntary national test proposed by President Clinton would follow a similar policy; some districts that had agreed to participate pulled out after they realized that the fourth grade reading test would be administered only in English.

As with accommodations for students with disabilities, the research on the effects of test accommodations for English-language learners is inconclusive. It is not always clear, for example, that different versions of tests in different languages are in fact measuring the same things (National Research Council, 1997b). Moreover, attempts to modify the language of tests—for example, simplifying directions—have not always made English-language tests easier to understand (Abedi, 1995).

One recent study of the effects of accommodations in a large-scale testing program, the state assessment in Rhode Island, found that the state's efforts to provide accommodations probably led to an increase in the number of English-language learners participating in the test and to gains in performance. However, the study concluded that the effects of the accommodations are uncertain, and that they may not work as intended (Shepard et al., 1998b).

Recommendations

- Teachers should regularly and frequently administer assessments, including assessments of English-language proficiency, for the purpose of monitoring the progress of English-language learners and for adapting instruction to improve performance.
- States and districts should develop clear guidelines for accommodations that permit English-language learners to participate in assessments administered for accountability purposes. Especially important are clear decision rules for determining the level of English-language proficiency at which English-language learners should be expected to participate exclusively in English-language assessments.
- Students should be assessed in the language that permits the most valid inferences about the quality of their academic performance. When numbers are sufficiently large, states and districts should develop subject-matter assessments in languages other than English.
- English-language learners should be exempted from assessments only when there is evidence that the assessment, even with accommodations, cannot measure the knowledge or skill of particular students or groups of students.
- States and districts should describe the methods they use to screen English-language learners for accommodations, exemptions, and alternate assessments, and they should report the frequency of these practices.
- Federal research units, foundations, and other funding agencies should promote research that advances knowledge about the validity and reliability of different accommodation, exemption, and alternate assessment practices for English-language learners.

Questions to Ask

❑ Are valid and reliable measures used to evaluate the level of students' proficiency in English?

❑ Are clear guidelines in place for accommodations that permit English-language learners to participate in assessments administered for accountability purposes? Are decision rules in place that enable determination of the level of English-language proficiency at which English-language learners should be expected to participate exclusively in English-language assessments?

❑ Is there evidence that the assessment, even with accommodations, cannot measure the knowledge or skill of particular students or groups of students before alternate assessments are administered?

❑ Are assessments provided in languages other than English when the numbers of students who can take such assessments is sufficiently large to warrant their use?

❑ Are the methods used to screen students to determine whether they need accommodations for tests reported, including the frequency of such practices?

riteria

Assessments for English-language learners should follow the same criteria used for assessments generally, which were described above. In addition, such assessments should also meet additional criteria based on the unique problems associated with testing English-language learners. The committee recommends that, in developing an assessment system for English-language learners, states and districts adhere to the following criteria:

Inclusion. The assessments should provide a means of including all students; they should be exempt only when assessments, even with accommodations, do not yield valid and reliable information about students' knowledge and skills. The state or district should provide accommodations for those who can participate in the regular assessment.

Appropriateness. States and districts need to ensure that accommodations meet the needs of students, and that tests administered under different conditions represent accurate measures of students' knowledge and skills.

Documentation. States and districts should develop and document policies regarding the basis for assigning accommodations to students and for reporting the results of students who have taken tests with accommodations.

xamples

The following examples show the practices of a district and a state that have clear policies for including English-language learners in assessments. Both use measures of English-language proficiency to determine whether students can take part in the regular assessment or use a native-language test or an accommodation. Both disaggregate test results to show performance of English-language learners who have taken native-language tests or tests with accommodations.

The Texas Assessment of Academic Skills (TAAS) is administered to every student in Texas in grades 3-8 and grade 10. The tests are used for both student and school accountability. For students, the 10th grade tests in reading, mathematics, and writing are designed as exit-level tests, which students must pass in order to graduate. For schools and districts, the tests are the centerpiece of a complex information and accountability system; schools are rated as "exemplary," "recognized," "acceptable," or "low-performing" on the basis of scores on the TAAS, attendance rates, and dropout rates.

The state also administers a Spanish-language version of the TAAS in grades 3-6.

To determine which version of the test students take, language-proficiency assessment committees at each school, consisting of a site administrator, a bilingual educator, an English-as-a-second-language educator, and a parent of a child currently enrolled, make judgments according to six criteria. These are: literacy in English and/or Spanish; oral-language proficiency in English and/or Spanish; academic program participation, language of instruction, and planned language of assessments; number of years continuously enrolled in the school; previous testing history; and level of academic achievement. On the basis of these criteria, the committee determines whether a student is tested on the English-language TAAS, tested on the Spanish-language TAAS, or is exempted and provided an alternate assessment. Those entering U.S. schools in the 3rd grade or later are required to take the English TAAS after three years.

The results for students who take the Spanish TAAS or for those who are exempted are not included in the totals used for accountability purposes; however, the Spanish-language results are reported for each school. In 1997, 2.4 percent of the students in grades 3-8 were exempted because of limited English proficiency; another 1.48 percent of students took the Spanish TAAS.

In Philadelphia, the district administers the Stanford Achievement Test-9th Form (SAT-9) as part of an accountability system; the results are used, along with attendance rates, to determine whether schools are making adequate progress in bringing students toward district standards. The district also administers the Spanish-language version of the SAT-9, known as Aprenda, in reading and mathematics.

To determine how students should be tested, the district measures the students' English-language proficiency. The district has used the Language Assessment Scales (LAS), a standard measure that gauges proficiency on a four-point scale; more recently, district educators have developed their own descriptors of language proficiency. The district is currently conducting research to compare the locally developed descriptors with the LAS.

Students at the lowest level of proficiency—those who are not literate in their native language—are generally exempted from the

SAT-9, as are recently arrived immigrants who are level 2 (beginner). Those in the middle levels of proficiency, level 2 (beginner) and level 3 (intermediate), who are instructed in bilingual programs, are administered Aprenda in reading and mathematics, and a translated SAT-9 open-ended test in science. Those in levels 2 and 3 who are not in bilingual programs take the SAT-9 with accommodations. Those at level 4 (advanced) take the SAT-9 with appropriate accommodations.

Accommodations include extra time; multiple shortened test periods; simplification of directions; reading aloud of questions (for mathematics and science); translation of words and phrases on the spot (for mathematics and science); decoding of words upon request (not for reading); use of gestures and nonverbal expressions to clarify directions and prompts; student use of graphic organizers and artwork; testing in a separate room or small-group setting; use of a study carrel; and use of a word-match glossary.

All students who take part in the assessment are included in school accountability reports. Those who are not tested receive a score of zero.

For schools eligible for Title I schoolwide status (those with high proportions of low-income students), the district is pilot-testing a performance assessment in reading and mathematics. The performance assessment may become part of the district's accountability system. Students at all levels of English proficiency participate in the performance assessment, with accommodations (National Research Council, 1999a).

REPORTING ASSESSMENT RESULTS

In many ways, reporting the results of tests is one of the most significant aspects of testing and assessment. Test construction, item development, and scoring are means of gathering information. It is the information, and the inferences drawn from the information, that makes a difference in the lives of students, parents, teachers, and administrators.

The traditional method of reporting test results is in reference to norms; that is, by comparing student performance to the performance of a national sample of students, called a norm group, who took the same test. Norm-referenced test scores help provide a context for the results by showing parents, teachers, and the public whether student performance is better or worse than that of others. This type of reporting may be useful for making selection decisions.

Norm-referenced reporting is less useful for providing information about what students know or are able to do. To cite a commonly used analogy, norm-referenced scores tell you who is farther up the mountain; they do not tell you how far anyone has climbed. For that type of information, criterion-referenced, or standards-referenced, reports are needed. These types of reports compare student performance to agreed-upon standards for what students should know and be able to do, irrespective of how other students performed.

It is important to note that the terms "norm-referenced" and "standards-referenced" are characteristics of reports, not tests. However, the type of report a test is intended to produce influences how it is designed. Tests designed to produce comparative scores generally omit items that nearly all students can answer or those that nearly all students cannot answer, since these items do not yield comparisons. Yet such items may be necessary for a standards-referenced report, if they measure student performance against standards.

Some of the ways test results are reported confound the distinction between norm-referenced and standards-referenced reporting. For example, many newspaper accounts and members of the public refer to "grade-level" or "grade-equivalent" scores as though these scores represent standards for students in a particular grade. That is, they refer to the scores as though they believe that, when 40 percent of students are reading "at grade-level," two-fifths of students are able to read what students in their grade are expected to read, based on shared judgments about expectations for student performance. In fact, "grade level" is a statistical concept that is calculated by determining the mean performance of a norm group for a given grade. Half of the students in the norm group necessarily perform "below grade level," if the test is properly normed.

Because of the interest among policy makers and the public for both types of information—information about comparative performance and performance against standards—several states combine standards-based reports with norm-referenced reports; similarly, states participate in the National Assessment of Educational Progress to provide comparative information as well.

By requiring states to "provide coherent information about student attainment of the state's content and student performance standards," the Title I statute effectively mandates the use of standards-based reports. The law also requires states to set at least three levels of achievement: proficient, advanced, and partially proficient. However, the law leaves open the possibility that states can provide norm-referenced information as well.

indings

Reporting results from tests according to standards depends first on decision rules about classifying students and schools. Creating those decision rules is a judgmental process, in which experts and lay people make decisions about what students at various levels of achievement ought to know and be able to do (Hambleton, 1998). One group's judgments may differ from another's. As a result, reports that indicate that a proportion of students are below the proficient level—not meeting standards—may not reflect the true state of student achievement. Another process may suggest that more students have in fact met standards (Mills and Jaeger, 1998).

The experience of the National Assessment Governing Board (NAGB) in setting achievement levels for the National Assessment of Educational Progress illustrates the challenges in making valid and reliable judgments about the levels of student performance. The NAGB achievement levels have received severe criticism over the years (National Research Council, 1998). Critics have found that the descriptions of performance NAGB uses to characterize "basic," "proficient," and "advanced" levels of achievement on NAEP do not correspond to student performance at each of the levels. Students who performed at the basic level could perform tasks intended to demonstrate proficient achievement, for example. Moreover, researchers have found that the overall levels appear to have been set too high, compared with student performance on other measures.

One issue surrounding the use of achievement levels relates to the precision of the estimates of the proportions of students performing at each level. Large margins of error could have important ramifications if the performance standards are used to reward or punish schools or school districts; a school with large numbers of students classified as "partially proficient" may in fact have a high proportion of students at the "proficient" level.

The risk of misclassification is particularly high when states and districts use more than one cutscore, or more than two levels of achievement, as NAEP does (Ragosa, 1994). However, other efforts have shown that it is possible to classify students' performance with a relatively high degree of accuracy and consistency (Young and Yoon, 1998). In any case, such classifications always contain some degree of statistical uncertainty; reports on performance should include data on the level of confidence with which the classification is made.

Another problem with standards-based reporting stems from the fact that tests generally contain relatively few items that measure performance against particular standards or groups of standards. While the test overall may be aligned with the standards, it may include only one or two items that measure performance on, say, the ability to identify the different types of triangles. Because student performance can vary widely from item to item, particularly with performance items, it would be inappropriate to report student results on each standard (Shavelson et al., 1993). As a result, reports that may be able to indicate whether students have attained standards can seldom indicate which standards students have attained. This limits their instructional utility, since the reports can seldom tell teachers which topic or skill a student needs to work on.

The challenges of reporting standards-based information are exacerbated with the use of multiple indicators. In some cases, the results for a student on two different measures could be quite different. For example, a student may perform well on a reading comprehension test but perform poorly on a writing assessment. This is understandable, since the two tests measure different skills; however, the apparent contradiction could appear confusing to the public (National Research Council, 1999b).

In an effort to help avoid such confusion and provide an overall measure of performance, many states have combined their multiple measures into a single index. Such indices enable states and districts to serve one purpose of test reporting: to classify schools in order to make judgments about their overall performance. However, the complex formulas states and districts use to calculate such indices make it difficult to achieve a second important purpose of reporting: to send cues about instructional improvement. Teachers and principals may have difficulty using the index to relate scores to performance or to classroom practices.

Recommendations

• Assessment results should be reported so that they indicate the status of student performance against standards.

• Performance levels of proficient or above should represent reasonable estimates of what students in a good instructional program can attain.

• Reports of student performance should include measures of statistical uncertainty, such as a confidence interval or the probability of misclassification.

• Reports of progress toward standards should include multiple indicators. When states and districts combine multiple indicators into a single index, they should report simultaneously the components of the index and the method used to compute it.

Questions to Ask

❑ Are assessment results reported according to standards?

❑ Is there a way to determine whether the proficient level of achievement represents a reasonable estimate of what students in a good program can attain, over time, with effort?

❑ Do reports indicate the confidence interval or probability of misclassification?

❑ Are multiple indicators used for reporting progress toward standards? When these indicators are combined into a single index, are the components of the index and the method used to compute it simultaneously reported?

Criteria

Relation to Standards. Assessment results provide the most useful information when they report student performance against standards. To the extent possible, reports indicating performance against particular standards or clusters of standards provide instructionally useful information.

Clarity. Reports that show in an understandable way how students performed in relation to standards are useful. Reports that combine information from various sources into a single index should include the more detailed information that makes up the index as well.

"Consumer Rights." Assessment reports should provide as much information as possible to students, teachers, parents, and the public, and they should also help users avoid misinterpretations. The reports should state clearly the limits of the information available and indicate the inferences that are appropriate.

xamples

Figure 4-1 is an example of a school report that was developed by the National Center for Research on Evaluation, Standards, and Student Testing for the Los Angeles Unified School District. It shows a range of information on student performance—including test scores, course taking, and graduation rates—along with contextual information about the qualifications of teachers and the students' background. The test the district uses includes norm-referenced reports rather than standards-referenced reports. In addition, the report does not indicate the degree of statistical uncertainty of the test scores.

FIGURE 4-1 School report for the Los Angeles Unified School District. Source: The National Center for Research on Evaluation, Standards and Student Testing (CRESST). Copyright 1999 by The Regents of the University of California and supported under the Office of Educational Research and Improvement (OERI), U.S. Department of Education. Used with permission.

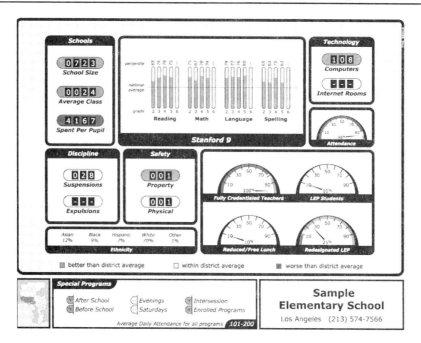

DISAGGREGATING DATA

In addition to reporting overall data on student performance, states and districts also disaggregate the data to show the performance of particular groups of students. The Title I statute requires states and districts to report the performance of students by race, gender, economic status, and other factors. This requirement was intended to ensure that states and districts do not neglect disadvantaged students.

Disaggregating data helps provide a more accurate picture of performance and makes it possible to use assessment data to improve performance. For example, one state examined two districts that had vastly different overall rates of performance. But when state officials broke out the data by race and poverty, they found that poor black students performed roughly equally in both districts. This finding suggested that the higher-performing district's overall scores reflected its success with the majority of students, not all students.

This kind of information can be quite powerful. Rather than rest on their laurels, the high-performing district can look for ways to adjust its instructional program for poor black students. That suggests a strategy that might not be apparent if the district looked only at overall results.

In addition, states and districts can use disaggregated results to see the effects of their policies and practices on various groups. It may be, for example, that implementing a new form of assessment without changing the conditions of instruction in all schools could widen the gap in performance between white and black students. By looking at results for different groups of students, districts and states can monitor the unintended effects of their policies and make needed changes.

indings

The idea of disaggregation stems in part from a substantial body of literature aimed at determining the effects of schooling on student performance (Raudenbush and Willms, 1995). These studies, which examined the variation in school performance after taking into account the background of the students in the schools, found that some schools do a better job than others in educating children, and the researchers have examined the characteristics of successful schools. However, as Willms (1998) points out, despite these findings, states and school districts continue to report misleading information about school performance by publishing overall average test scores, without taking into account the range of performance within a school.

Overall averages can be misleading because the variation in performance *within* schools is much greater than the variation *among* schools (Willms, 1998). That is, to take a hypothetical example, the difference between the performance of white students and black students in School A is much greater than the difference between School A's performance and School B's performance. Simply reporting the schools' overall performance, without showing the differences within the schools, could lead to erroneous conclusions about the quality of instruction in each school. And if districts took action based on those conclusions, the remedies might be inappropriate and perhaps harmful.

Breaking down assessment results into results for smaller groups increases the statistical uncertainty associated with the results, and affects the inferences drawn from the results. This is particularly true with small groups of students. For example, consider a school of 700 students, of whom 30 are black. A report that disaggregates test scores by race would indicate the performance of the 30 black students. Although this result would accurately portray the performance of these particular students, it would be inappropriate to say the results show how well the school educates black students. Another group of black students could perform quite differently (Jaeger and Tucker, 1998).

In addition, states and districts need to be careful if groups are so small that individual students can be identified. A school with just two American Indian students in 4th grade risks violating the students' privacy if it reports an average test score for American Indian students.

Disaggregated results can also pose challenges if results are compared from year to year. If a state tests 4th grade students each year, its assessment reports will indicate the proportion of students in 4th grade in 1999 at the proficient level compared with the proportion of 4th graders in 1998 at that level. But the students are not the same each year, and breaking down results by race, gender, and other categories increases the sampling error. Reports that show performance declining from one year to the next may reflect differences in the student population more than differences in instructional practice.

Recommendations

- States, districts, and schools should disaggregate data to ensure that schools will be accountable for the progress of all children, especially those with the greatest educational needs.
- Schools should report data so that it is possible to determine the performance of economically disadvantaged students and English-language learners.
- In reporting disaggregated data, states and districts should report the associated confidence levels.

Questions to Ask

❏ Do schools collect and report data on performance of all groups within each school, particularly economically disadvantaged students and English-language learners?

❏ Are there methods for determining the margin of error associated with disaggregated data?

Criteria

Comprehensiveness. Breaking out test results by race, gender, income, and other categories enhances the quality of the data and provides a more complete picture of achievement in a school or district.

Accuracy. In order to enhance the quality of inferences about achievement drawn from the data, states and districts need to reveal the extent of error and demonstrate how that error affects the results.

Privacy. When groups of students are so small that there is a risk of violating their privacy, the results for these groups should not be reported.

Example

The following example describes the practice in a state that disaggregates test data for each school and uses the disaggregated data to hold schools accountable for performance.

> Under the Texas accountability system, the state rates districts each year in four categories—exemplary, recognized, academically acceptable, and academically unacceptable—and rates schools as exemplary, recognized, acceptable, and low-performing. The ratings are based on student performance on the state test, the Texas Assessment of Academic Skills, the dropout rate, and the attendance rate. In order to earn a coveted "exemplary" or "recognized" rating, districts or schools must not only have a high overall passing rate on the TAAS, a low overall dropout rate, and a high overall attendance rate, but the rates for each group within a school or district—African Americans, Hispanics, whites, and economically disadvantaged students under the state's designations—must also exceed the standard for each category. Schools that might have met the requirements for a high rating because of high average performance but fell short because of relatively low performance by students from a particular group have focused their efforts on improving the lagging group's performance—a response that might not have taken place if they had not disaggregated the results.

CHAPTER 5

Monitoring the Conditions of Instruction

The theory of standards-based reform suggests that if states set challenging standards for students, measure student progress toward the standards, and hold schools accountable for meeting those targets, schools will make the adjustments in curriculum and instruction necessary to bring all students to the standards.

This theory was aimed at achieving a balancing act. On one hand, advocates argued for the need for common standards for all students and common assessments that would gauge student learning against the standards. But on the other hand, the architects of standards-based reform also wanted to honor teachers' professional knowledge and judgment. Within the framework of common goals for students, the designers of the new systems set out to provide flexibility for teachers to enable them to meet the particular needs of their students.

In practice, though, the theory ended up placing a heavy burden on teachers and other school professionals. Districts were supposed to provide teachers with models of effective instructional practice and support for developing and strengthening their curriculum and instructional techniques, but many lacked the wherewithal to do so effectively. Although the theory of standards-based reform placed great emphasis on what students should know and be able to do, it remained silent about the knowledge and skills needed for teachers.

As a result, the states and districts that have implemented standards-based systems have seen a familiar pattern. In the first few years, as teachers become aware of the new systems and make some adjustments to their classrooms, performance increases, in some cases substantially. However, performance then flattens and hits a plateau unless districts and states make concerted efforts to provide the support needed to develop the capacity of teachers to teach to the new standards.

THE CONDITIONS OF INSTRUCTION

Findings

In many respects, the demands for standards for student performance and new forms of assessment are aimed at fostering changes in teaching, particularly for low-income students. Critics argued that the kind of didactic, teacher-directed instruction that traditionally characterized American classrooms did not lead to the high levels of learning the reformers wanted to encourage. And many argued that traditional tests encouraged teachers to place a premium on quick recall, rather than on solving problems in real-world contexts (Resnick and Resnick, 1992; Shepard, 1991).

Other studies, particularly in international research, showed that the type of teaching students were exposed to was linked to their achievement; simply put, students learned what they were taught (Schmidt et al., 1998). However, a number of studies had found gaps between the curriculum taught in schools with large numbers of low-income students and that taught in schools with more affluent students: the more affluent students were more likely to receive challenging assignments than their lower-income peers (Puma et al., 1997; Smith et al., 1998).

Newmann and Associates labeled the kind of instruction reformers advocated for all students "authentic pedagogy," and found that such practices were associated with higher levels of achievement. By authentic pedagogy, Newmann and Associates referred to the following standards (1996:33):

- **Higher-Order Thinking**. Instruction involves students in manipulating information and ideas by synthesizing, generalizing, explaining, hypothesizing, or arriving at conclusions that produce new meaning and understandings for them.
- **Deep Knowledge**. Instruction addresses central ideas of a topic or discipline with enough thoroughness to explore connections and relationships and to produce relatively complex understandings.
- **Substantive Conversation**. Students engage in extended conversational exchanges with the teacher or their peers about subject matter in a way that builds an improved and shared understanding of ideas or topics.
- **Connections to the World Beyond the Classroom**. Students make connections between substantive knowledge and either public problems or personal experiences.

The small body of research that has examined classrooms in depth suggests that such instructional practices may be rare, even among teachers who say they endorse the changes the standards are intended to foster. In one study of 25 teachers in Michigan, James P. Spillane found that all teachers said they attended closely to the state policy and reported that it affected their teaching. But when he looked inside their classrooms, only 4 had fundamentally changed the kinds of tasks students were expected to perform and the discourse in their classroom (the study examined mathematics teaching and learning). In 11 classrooms, there was no indication that the tasks and discourse had changed at all (Spillane, 1997).

In large part, Spillane found, the discrepancy reflected the variation in teachers' understanding about the tests' instructional goals. For example, teachers saw that the test put a premium on problem solving, but for some, that meant adding a word problem at the end of each lesson. This variation in understanding was true among principals and district office staff as well.

A separate study of 22 classrooms in 6 states found a similar pattern (David, 1997). In examining teachers' responses to new assessments, David distinguishes between "imitation" and "improvement." Most teachers imitated the form of the new assessment, she found, often by adding open-ended questions to their classroom assessments or assigning more writing. But these responses produced limited results. By contrast, she noted, some teachers went beyond imitation and changed their practice fundamentally.

Districts' capacity to monitor the conditions of instruction in schools is limited, and there are few examples of districts that have been shown to be effective in analyzing such conditions and using the data to improve instruction. The research base on such efforts is slim, in large part because there are so few examples to study.

The examples begin to suggest, however, that examining instructional practices, along with data on performance, and using that information to develop a professional development strategy, can help teachers improve their instruction and help improve student performance.

• In Brazosport, Texas, the district established instructional specialists and facilitators, who observed teachers in classrooms, then worked with them to help analyze data on student performance and model lessons and instructional strategies. The facilitators often helped teachers learn new techniques by teaching lessons themselves and showing the teachers that their students were capable of learning more than they had thought they could (Ragland et al., 1999).

• Community District 2 in New York City has created a Supervisory Goals and Objectives process that focuses principals' and district administrators' attention on instruction and ways to improve it. The principals develop annual plans for instructional improvement, which form the basis for performance reviews by administrators. The administrators—including the superintendent and deputy superintendent—visit schools frequently, observing classrooms and meeting with the principal to discuss improvement strategies. The district has also organized a number of professional development models that schools can use (Elmore, 1997).

• In Philadelphia, the district has established Teaching and Learning Networks in each "cluster" of schools. The network staffs visit schools and work with teachers to develop professional development strategies based on performance and instructional needs (Wang et al., 1999).

Recommendations

• Schools and districts should monitor the conditions of instruction—the curriculum and instructional practices of teachers—to determine if students are exposed to teaching that would enable them to achieve the standards they are expected to meet.

• Districts and schools should use information on the conditions of instruction to require and support improvement of instruction and learning in every classroom.

• Teachers should use the information on conditions of instruction in their classroom, along with data on student performance, to improve the quality of instruction. Districts have a responsibility to assist schools in collecting and using such information.

• Schools should use the information on the conditions of instruction to organize the time and resources provided to teachers and demand support from the district.

• Districts should use the information on the conditions of instruction to improve the quality and effectiveness of the resources and support they provide to schools for instructional improvement.

Questions to Ask

❑ Are curriculum and instructional practices monitored in schools?

❑ Do schools use data about curriculum and instructional practices, along with performance data, to develop plans for instructional improvement?

❑ Are data about curriculum and instructional practices, along with performance data, used to strengthen the support provided to schools for instructional improvement?

Criteria

Relationship to Student Standards. The data on classroom practices should be examined against the expectations for student performance embodied in the state or district standards. Instruction should enable students to achieve the standards.

Coherence. The conditions of instruction should be consistent within schools and across grades. Students should be exposed to the same content and instructional practices if they are expected to achieve the same standards.

Disaggregation. Data on instructional practices should be reported by race, gender, socioeconomic status, and other factors to indicate whether all students in schools are exposed to similar conditions of instruction.

xamples

The following two examples are efforts by researchers to examine the conditions of instruction in Chicago public schools. In one, the researchers administered an extensive survey and conducted detailed observations of classrooms. In the other, the researchers examined student assignments—the work students performed as part of their daily classroom activities. In both cases, the researchers viewed their findings against standards for effective instruction.

To find out about the conditions of instruction in the Chicago Public Schools, researchers from the Consortium on Chicago School Research conducted an extensive survey of teachers and students in 1994 and analyzed the information from 2,036 teachers. Researchers then observed over 800 language arts and mathematics classes in eight elementary schools and seven high schools. They analyzed classroom lessons against the subject-matter content of the test used in the district, the Iowa Tests of Basic Skills.

The researchers found that many Chicago classrooms keep pace with grade-level expectations and test content, but many others do not. As a result, many students do not learn the content they need in order to perform well on the tests. "Especially troublesome," the researchers write, "is the finding that students attending schools in Chicago's most disadvantaged neighborhoods are much more likely to encounter instruction that is poorly coordinated and that conveys weak expectations for student learning" (p. 1).

The study found, for example, that although instruction in early grades tends to follow the expectations of the test, the pacing flattens out by about fourth grade, particularly in high-poverty schools, and classes tend to repeat topics already taught. And the repeated lessons do not build on prior learning; rather, the lessons tend to repeat the same basic skills students were exposed to before. In some cases, elementary lessons were more demanding than those in middle or high school. The pattern exists in language arts instruction as well: there, they found, students might read more challenging books in higher grades, but they are not asked to explore them in any more depth than they were when they were younger.

The results suggest, the researchers conclude, that many Chicago youngsters are not exposed to the knowledge and skills they will be tested on (Smith et al., 1998).

A separate study, also in Chicago, examined student assignments in writing and mathematics in grades 3, 6, and 8 in 12 schools. The researchers analyzed the assignments and student work against standards for intellectual quality. These standards emphasize the construction of knowledge, or the ability to apply or extend knowledge to new situations; the use of disciplined inquiry, or the ability to build on prior knowledge, strive for in-depth understanding, and communicate their understanding; and the value beyond school, or the extent to which student learning has an impact on others besides the demonstration of competence.

The study found that the majority of assignments at all grade levels represented no challenge or minimal challenge. And they found that students who were assigned more challenging work were better able to perform at higher levels. They conclude that, although the unchallenging and minimally challenging assignments may enable students to learn basic facts and procedures, they do not equip them to do the kind of tasks they might be expected to perform as workers and citizens outside school (Newmann et al., 1998).

PROFESSIONAL DEVELOPMENT

 indings

Just as students' achievement is related to what they are taught, teachers, too, are able to transform their instructional practice when they have had opportunities for sustained learning in new instructional approaches. As David notes in her study of teachers' responses to new forms of assessment, teacher learning represented the difference between imitation and improvement. She writes (David, 1997, p. 12):

Teachers who described changes in their practices, beyond introducing a new lesson or activity here or there, usually point to a combination of experiences leading to these changes. These include extensive and repeated opportunities for learning that (a) cause teachers to think about and know content differently; and (b) provide a range of teaching strategies and curriculum ideas. The most influential of these opportunities usually combine one week or longer summer institutes over successive years in which teachers are learning new content in a particular subject area (e.g., literacy or mathematics) in the ways they will be teaching it, coupled with access to help during the school day from staff developers, administrators, and colleagues.

Yet such transformation on a large scale has occurred rarely, if at all (Elmore, 1996). The isolation in which teachers work—isolation from one another, as well as to the world outside their schools—hinders their ability to examine their practices against external yardsticks and learn about new practices.

States and districts have traditionally attempted to provide such experiences for teachers through professional development. But the amount of professional development that states and districts provide may be inadequate, and the quality varies widely. A national survey of teachers found that, although nearly all teachers participated in professional development in 1998, most of these activities lasted from 1 to 8 hours, or less than a full day (National Center for Education Statistics, 1999). Significantly, the survey found, teachers who spent more than 8 hours in professional development were more likely than those who spent less time in such activities to say that such learning improved their classroom teaching.

Not all professional development opportunities are equally valuable. A common format, workshops or conferences, are not considered effective in producing change in teaching practices or student learning (Fullan with Stiegelbauer, 1991). Such formats tend to be short-term events, isolated from the context in which teachers teach, with few opportunities for sustained interaction with peers or experts.

The National Partnership for Excellence and Accountability in Teaching, a consortium of organizations conducting research on teacher preparation and practice, has synthesized research on professional development and developed eight principles for effective practices (1999):

• Professional development should be based on analyses of the differences between (a) actual student performance and (b) the goals and standards for student learning.

• Professional development should involve teachers in the identification of what they need to learn and in the development of the learning experiences in which they will be involved.

• Professional development should be primarily school-based and built into the day-to-day work of teaching.

• Professional development should be organized around collaborative problem solving.

• Professional development should be continuous and ongoing, involving follow-up and support for further learning—including support from sources external to the school that can provide necessary resources and new perspectives.

• Professional development should incorporate evaluation of multiple sources of information on (a) outcomes for students and (b) the instruction and other processes that are involved in implementing the lessons learned through professional development.

- Professional development should provide opportunities to gain an understanding of the theory underlying the knowledge and skills being learned.
- Professional development should be connected to a comprehensive change process focusing on improving student learning.

Other research suggests that the content of professional development is related to its effectiveness. The most effective subject of professional development appears to be focused on the content teachers teach. In one major study of teachers in California, teachers who participated in learning opportunities focused on the curriculum—lessons they were teaching—were more likely to change their practice than those who participated in sessions dealing with special topics, like cooperative learning or diversity, that are more abstract and less directly related to the content the teachers teach (Cohen and Hill, 1998). Moreover, the curriculum-based professional development also appeared to affect student learning: students whose teachers participated in curriculum sessions outperformed others on the state test. Significantly, however, the study found, teachers' opportunities for professional development varied. Teachers of more affluent students were more likely than teachers of disadvantaged students to take part in the curriculum workshops, and teachers of disadvantaged students participated in the special topics workshops more often.

Other areas of professional development that appear to have an impact on changing practice are activities centered on student assessment. In Kentucky and Vermont, portfolios in mathematics and writing have had a strong influence on instruction (Stecher et al., 1998; Koretz, et al., 1996). Teachers say that training in scoring portfolios has helped them understand the characteristics of high-quality work and the teaching strategies that help to produce such work. Teachers also report that scoring performance assessments has had the same effect.

However, researchers have found that teachers have had few opportunities to learn about classroom assessment—the frequent assessments they undertake to monitor their students' progress over the course of the year. Teacher preparation programs provide little emphasis on measurement (Plake and Impara, 1997), and most instruction in measurement focuses on technical assessment issues, rather than strategies for gauging student progress (Calfee and Masuda, 1997). Largely as a result, teachers say they feel inadequately prepared in assessment (Aschbacher, 1994).

Recommendations

- Districts should design professional development that is focused on the standards for student performance.
- Districts should use results from student assessments and

information on conditions of instruction to design their professional development programs.

   • Districts should review the quality and impact of their professional development offerings and revise them if they do not lead to improvements in teaching practice or student performance.

Questions to Ask

❏Are professional development offerings related to the standards for student performance?

❏Are results from student assessments and information on conditions of instruction used to design professional development programs?

❏Are the quality and impact of professional development offerings reviewed and revised if they do not lead to improvements in teaching practice or student performance?

Criteria

Link Between Assessment and Instruction. The more sensitive assessments are to instructional change, the more likely they will influence practice. Such assessments provide a signal to teachers and principals about what they need to change and provide information about the effects of their actions on student achievement.

Focus on Student Work. Professional development that examines student work in relation to standards—such as training for scoring performance assessments or portfolios—provides a clear picture of the kind of work students who attain standards should perform and the classroom activities that can enable students to produce such work regularly. Such opportunities make the often-abstract language of standards more concrete.

Focus on Content Standards. Professional development that focuses on the content teachers are expected to teach, rather than on generic topics that may not be related to the standards students should achieve, helps teachers understand how to redesign their practice. Such professional development emphasizes not only the content knowledge teachers are expected to have but also "pedagogical content knowledge"—the knowledge they need to teach the content to students. Such professional development models the link between standards and instructional practice by working with teachers to figure out how the standards apply in their classrooms.

Examples

The following two examples describe states and a district where professional development is linked directly to instructional improvement. In the case of Community District 2, the district monitors the professional development efforts closely.

Portfolio systems in place in Kentucky and Vermont have proven to be powerful tools in improving instruction—particularly in writing—in both states. In Kentucky, the state assessment (until 1998) required each student in each grade tested to compile a portfolio of work completed during the course of the school year in writing and mathematics. The mathematics portfolio was required to include five to seven best pieces that show an understanding of core concepts, using a variety of mathematical tools. The writing portfolio, depending on the grade level, was required to include pieces from several content areas. Students were required to include a table of contents and a letter commenting on the work.

Teachers scored the portfolios. They received scoring guides, benchmarks, and training portfolios, and the state and districts provided training in standards and scoring procedures. According to one survey, two-thirds of 5th- and 8th-grade teachers said they had received training in preparing students for the mathematics portfolios, and 85 percent of 4th- and 7th-grade teachers said they had received training related to the writing portfolios (Stecher et al., 1998).

By several accounts, the portfolios and the related professional development have had an impact on instruction. A number of studies found that the amount of writing students do has increased substantially, and that the practices teachers employ in teaching and evaluating student writing have changed significantly. Writing performance rose substantially in 4th grade (although it leveled off), somewhat in 8th grade, and remained flat in 12th grade.

In Vermont, the first state to include portfolios as part of a statewide assessment system, the story is similar. There, students are required to compile a portfolio that includes five to seven pieces completed during the course of a year, a "best piece," and a letter commenting on the choices. Samples of the portfolios are scored centrally by trained teachers, and the results are reported for the state.

The state provides professional development for teachers around the portfolios, and between two-thirds and four-fifths of teachers participated in at least one professional development activity (Picus and Tralli, 1998).

As in Kentucky, teachers in Vermont say the portfolio has had a positive influence on their instruction. Teachers in particular noted an increased attention to teaching writing and mathematical communication (Koretz et al., 1996; Picus and Tralli, 1998).

New York City's Community District 2 built its entire reform strategy around professional development. As Elmore (1997) writes, professional development in the district "is a management strategy rather than a specified administrative function. Professional development is what administrative leaders do when they are doing their jobs, not a specialized function that some people in the organization do and others don't. Instructional improvement is the main purpose of district administration, and professional development is the chief means of achieving that purpose" (p. 14).

As a result, monitoring instructional improvement efforts is part of the regular oversight function of the district. Each principal completes an annual plan that lays out the school's objectives and strategies for meeting the objectives, based on a structure laid out by district staff. The plans focus on instructional improvement in content areas and professional development activities for attaining the instructional improvement goals. The superintendent and deputy superintendent also visit each school at least once a year to observe instructional practices and discuss problems with the principal.

For its part, the district also provides an array of opportunities for professional development that schools can take part in. As part of its strategy, the district has arranged for specific consultants who meet district objectives; schools can select from among this array. In addition, the district spends about 3 percent of its annual budget on professional development, a figure that is probably higher than many other districts spend, although comparable figures are difficult to obtain (Elmore, 1997).

CHAPTER 6

Adequate Yearly Progress

In addition to requiring states to set standards for student performance, the 1994 Title I statute also calls on states to determine whether schools are making "adequate yearly progress" in bringing students up to the standards they have set. Specifically, the law states that adequate yearly progress must be defined "in a manner that (1) results in continuous and substantial yearly improvement of each school and local education agency sufficient to achieve the goal of all children...meeting the state's proficient and advanced levels of achievement; [and] (2) is sufficiently rigorous to achieve that goal within an appropriate timeframe."

In this aspect, as in many others, the law represents a substantial departure from past practice. To be sure, Title I has long required some demonstration of improvement in performance. The Hawkins-Stafford Amendments of 1988, for example, required school districts to identify schools that failed to demonstrate progress and to develop improvement plans for such schools (Natriello and McDill, 1999). However, these provisions required schools only to show an upward trend, not to set a goal of enabling all students to reach challenging standards. And in many cases the requirements for improvement were modest; in some districts, any improvement at all was considered adequate.

The new law, by contrast, requires states to set a clear goal for all students, and requires evidence of progress toward that goal. Moreover, the requirement for the "appropriate timeframe" suggests that small steps toward the goal may not be enough. Steady, substantial improvement toward reaching the standards is necessary.

Defining and measuring adequate yearly progress poses enormous challenges. Because the concept is central to accountability—schools that fail to demonstrate adequate yearly progress will be subject to intervention or other remedies—determining when progress is adequate and measuring it accurately and fairly become critical. Improper designations or inaccurate measures could mean that schools that are making progress receive intervention inappropriately, or that students in schools that need help may not get the assistance they require.

ADEQUATE YEARLY PROGRESS

indings

The most common method states and districts have used to determine adequate yearly progress is to set a goal for school performance, determine how long it will take to meet the goal, define progress toward the goal, and determine how school results will be structured so that the state or district could evaluate a school's rate of progress (Carlson, 1996). One of the best-known examples of this approach is the method used in Kentucky, which has been applied in some form in a number of other states and districts.

Under Kentucky's system, the state set the overall target for all schools at the level at which all students perform at the proficient level and called this level 100. They then determined each school's baseline performance, based on the results of the initial administration of the state test—giving greater weight to students at the proficient and distinguished (advanced) levels than to those at lower levels of performance—and subtracted that score from 100. They then set each school's two-year target at 10 percent of the difference between the initial score and 100. At that rate, state officials reasoned, every school would reach the target within 20 years.

This approach depends heavily on the quality of the measures of school performance. As noted in Chapter 4, using average scores to determine school performance can provide misleading inferences. (Although Kentucky uses a weighted average, assigning different values to students at different points on the distribution, it fails to disaggregate the results or to account in some other way for the student population in each school.) The risk of misleading inferences is significant in measures of growth. As Willms (1998) points out, schools with high initial test scores tend to grow at a faster rate than those with lower initial scores. In part this phenomenon reflects the fact that high performance tends to be associated with high levels of parental support, fewer disciplinary problems, and high teacher quality—all of which can contribute to performance improvement. At a minimum, this finding suggests, comparisons of growth rates that do not take into account the composition of the school's student body may be misleading.

A second factor in the "gap-closing" model, as the Kentucky approach is sometimes called, is a theory about the expected rate of growth. The Kentucky method appears to assume a linear rate—each school will grow at a 10 percent rate every two years. There is little evidence to suggest that this assumption is valid, or indeed what rate might be expected. Kentucky's own experience shows that, after initial gains, improvement appears to have reached something of a plateau. Without evidence about the rate of progress that schools are capable of demonstrating, particularly schools with high proportions of low-income students, a gap-closing model might set up unrealistic expectations and could provoke a backlash among schools that fail to meet such expectations.

Another design issue in the development of measures of progress is related to the frequency of assessment. Kentucky elected not to test students in every grade level and instead relies on cross-sectional measures. That is, in determining progress, the state compares this year's 4th graders with last year's. This may be misleading, particularly in small schools, since the population of students in a school may differ significantly from one year to the next. Kentucky attempted to deal with this problem by gauging schools over a two-year period; year-to-year fluctuations in student populations could be ironed out over two years.

An alternative is to use longitudinal measures, which show the performance of one group of students over time. This approach is expensive, since it requires annual testing of each student and tracking of students who move from school to school (Carlson, 1996). And it tends to rely on traditional forms of testing, because of cost and the scaling of results. Performance measures tend to be more expensive than traditional multiple-choice tests, and annual testing of each student with performance measures would add up. In addition, performance measures often rate student performance according to qualitative characteristics, which are difficult to place on a linear scale—yet a linear scale might be needed to show growth from year to year (Baker and Linn, 1997).

A final design issue relates to the use of multiple measures. The Kentucky model uses an index that combines scores from all subject-area assessments, plus other data (such as dropout rates and attendance rates) into a single number. This method has the advantage of incorporating information from a range of indicators, so that judgments about progress do not rest on a single test. Schools can compensate for weak performance in one area by showing strong progress in another. Yet this system is highly complex, and few people understand how the index is compiled (Elmore et al., 1996). It fails to include the more detailed information about the data that constitute the index, to provide clues to educators about what to do to improve the next time.

Moreover, the index approach may exclude other data that may be useful in determining school progress toward standards. As noted in Chapter 5, data about classroom practices and the conditions of instruction are critical pieces of information in an educational improvement system. For one thing, they provide a context for the performance data, by showing whether any performance gains are accompanied by improvements in practice and support for instruction. In addition, the information about the conditions of instruction also can serve as "leading indicators" that provide evidence of progress in advance of progress on tests and other performance measures, in the same way that data on factory orders show growth in the economy in advance of increases in the employment rate.

Recommendations

- Measures of adequate yearly progress should include a range of indicators, including indicators of instructional quality as well as student outcomes.
- Measures of adequate yearly progress should include disaggregated results by race, gender, economic status, and other characteristics of the student population.
- The criterion for adequate yearly progress should be based on evidence from the highest-performing schools with significant proportions of disadvantaged students.

Questions to Ask

❏ Are data on the conditions of instruction as well as student outcomes collected and reported in the measures of school progress? Are these data disaggregated by race, gender, economic status, and other factors?

❏ Are data collected on school performance over time from high-performing schools with significant proportions of disadvantaged students to determine expectations for adequate progress for all schools?

Criteria

Moving the Distribution. The goal should be to enable all students to reach the desired level; therefore, any definition of progress should include success in reducing the number of students at the lower levels of achievement as well as increasing the number attaining the standards.

Continuous Progress. Progress measurements should encourage all schools to improve continuously; however, states should acknowledge schools that reach high levels of achievement.

Reduction of Error. If states in their adequate progress measures use cross-sectional measures of achievement—comparing this year's 4th graders to last year's—they should measure progress over at least a two-year period, in order to reduce the sampling error that could occur because of shifts in student populations in schools. If states assess each student each year and measure progress annually, they should measure performance of all students, not just those who happened to remain in a school from year to year.

Use of Multiple Measures. Because of the limitations of test scores, measures of progress should not rely on single tests only, but should combine information from a range of sources. However, this information should be combined in ways that are transparent and understandable to schools and the public.

Regular Review. In order to ensure that the criteria for determining progress remain valid and that the method for determining school progress remains sound, states and districts should regularly review the reliability, validity, and utility of the overall system and revise the technical specifications and performance expectations when appropriate.

xamples

The following examples are from two states that meet some, but not all, of the committee's criteria for adequate yearly progress. North Carolina's system uses evidence from past performance in determining whether schools are eligible for recognition or for assistance. However, the state's criteria rely solely on test performance, rather than on the use of multiple measures, and it judges school performance based on average performance, rather than on the performance of subgroups within schools. Missouri's system for determining adequate progress, meanwhile, explicitly encourages schools to narrow the achievement gap between high-performing and low-performing students, not just raise the overall average. But the state's system relies only on test performance and does not base its targets on evidence from successful schools.

> North Carolina judges the progress of schools by examining scores on the state's End of Course tests and compiling a "growth composite" that is based on three factors: statewide average growth, the previous performance of students in the school, and a statistical adjustment which is needed whenever test scores of students are compared from one year to the next.
>
> The state provides cash awards to schools that show substantial gains in performance. Schools gaining at the "expected" rate, based on the state formula, receive awards of up to $750 per certified staff member and $375 per teaching assistant. Schools that register "exemplary" gains, or 10 percent above the statewide average, can receive up to $1,500 for each certified staff member and $500 per teaching assistant. Schools can use the money for bonuses for teachers or for school programs. Schools must test at least 95 percent of their students (98 percent in grades K-8) in order to be eligible for recognition.

In 1998, Missouri began to implement a new assessment system, known as the Missouri Assessment Program (MAP), that is designed to measure progress on the state standards. The program consists of assessments in mathematics, communications arts, and science; social studies, health and physical education, and fine arts are expected to be added in the coming years. The state board of education has designated five levels of performance on the assessment—"advanced," "proficient," "nearing proficient," "progressing," and "step 1" (lowest).

To meet the criterion for adequate yearly progress under Title I, schools must reduce the number of low-performing students. Specifically, schools must achieve one of the following:

• At least a 5 percent increase in the composite percentage of students in the upper three performance levels and at least a 5 percent decrease in the percentage of students in the bottom performance level;

• A 20 percent decrease in the percent of students in the bottom performance level, in schools in which at least 40 percent of a class group is represented in the bottom level;

• The percentage of students in the bottom performance level is 5 percent or less.

CHAPTER 7

Accountability

One of the most prominent issues in education policy today, accountability is a key element in the success of education improvement systems. Literally the process by which students, teachers, and administrators *give an account of* their progress, accountability is a means by which policy makers at the state and district levels—and parents and taxpayers—monitor the performance of students and schools. Accountability systems include a range of mechanisms, from simply requiring schools and districts to report on progress to policy makers and the public, to placing consequences—rewards for high performance and sanctions for poor performance—on the results of performance measures.

The 1994 Title I statute includes a number of provisions regarding the establishment of accountability structures. The law requires states to develop measures to determine whether schools are making adequate yearly progress toward the standards, based on the state assessments. It also states that local education agencies shall designate as "distinguished" schools that exceed the state's definition of adequate yearly progress for three consecutive years, and that such schools can be rewarded with Title I funds. At the same time, the law states, local education agencies shall identify schools that fail to make adequate progress and target them for assistance; after three years, such schools are subject to "corrective action," including the loss of funds, reconstitution of the staff, and the transfer of students.

By focusing on student performance as the measure by which schools and districts will be accountable to states, the 1994 statute reflects a substantial shift in thinking about accountability that has taken place over the past decade (Elmore et al., 1996). In the past, states held schools accountable for following rules set out by legislatures and boards of education, and for spending funds according to those rules. To that end, accountability mechanisms focused on inputs—the number of books in the library, the ratio of certified staff to students. These efforts were designed to ensure that schools carried out the mandates issued by state officials.

The new approaches shift the focus to outcomes—the results of all the inputs—and specifically to student achievement outcomes. These new systems reflect what the National Governors' Association (1986) referred to as a "horse trade": flexibility in exchange for accountability. Believing that those closest to students—schools and districts—knew best how to meet the needs of their student populations, the governors agreed to the idea of relaxing rules and giving schools maximum flexibility to design appropriate instructional programs. However, they said they would do so only so long as the schools produced results, and the states agreed that they would monitor the results, reward improvement, and impose sanctions for failure.

These new accountability schemes were designed to change the incentive structure for teachers and administrators. By placing consequences on the results, accountability was aimed at encouraging teachers and administrators to innovate and to design effective curricular and instructional programs that will improve student performance.

In addition, the accountability mechanisms were aimed at improving the efficiency and effectiveness of state agencies. By determining which schools are succeeding in their basic mission and which schools are failing, states could direct resources and assistance to the schools and districts that need them the most—the ones in which performance measures indicate problems. Otherwise, resources could be wasted, and needs could remain unmet. Students and taxpayers would both benefit under the new systems.

But designing a means of accountability poses a number of challenges. Chief among them is how schools respond to the accountability pressures. The external accountability structures can set ground rules and design incentives, but these processes will have the desired effect only if the *internal* accountability matches that from the outside. That is, teachers and administrators must hold themselves accountable for the performance of themselves and their students. If there is a mismatch between the internal and external accountability, when accountability knocks, no one may be home.

ACCOUNTABILITY

 indings

Who Is Accountable? One of the key design issues in accountability is determining who is to be held accountable. The Title I statute clearly intends for states to hold institutions—schools and school districts—accountable for student performance. Although the law requires states to collect and report data on individual students, its requirements for identifying schools and districts that have students exceeding (or failing to reach) standards place the locus of accountability on institutions, not individual students or teachers.

In doing so, the law follows the lead of early reforming states, such as Kentucky and Mississippi, that designed mechanisms explicitly for school and district accountability. The argument in those states was that school faculty and staffs, collectively, are responsible for student performance. Although a 4th grade teacher may determine to a large extent what a 4th grade student learns, and how that student performs on a 4th grade test, the student's performance in fact reflects the cumulative knowledge and skills she has learned to that point. Thus all teachers contribute to the students' achievement.

Moreover, school-level accountability was designed to encourage teachers to work together to improve instruction, in contrast to programs such as merit pay, which were seen as fostering competition among school staffs (Clotfelter and Ladd, 1996).

However, placing accountability at the school level may mask some important information. As Willms (1998) found, the variation in student performance *within* schools was greater than the variations *among* schools; therefore, reports that made judgments about school performance based only on overall results, without taking into account the variations within schools, could be misleading, since some teachers perform well and some perform poorly.

In addition, placing accountability at the school and district levels leaves out a key piece of the student performance puzzle—the students themselves. Some critics argue that such schemes set up a conflict of interest between students and teachers; teachers have a strong incentive to raise performance, but students, with nothing riding on the results, have little incentive to do their best on the tests, particularly at the high school level. This situation, moreover, reinforces the low levels of motivation high school students have to work hard in school, and masks the consequences for inadequate performance students will face when they get out of school and find themselves unable to find a high-paying job (Bishop, 1994).

In an effort to increase student motivation for schoolwork and hold students accountable for their own learning, a number of policy makers, including President Clinton, have proposed some form of student accountability, such as making promotion from grade to grade or graduation from high school contingent on demonstrating a certain level of performance, usually by passing a test. President Clinton and others have posed the issue as one of ending "social promotion," or the practice of moving students up the grades to remain with their peers, regardless of their academic performance. As the president stated in his 1998 State of the Union Address: "when we promote a child from grade to grade who hasn't mastered the work, we don't do the child any favors."

But as a number of studies have shown, schools do children no favors when they retain them in grade and continue to provide them with inadequate instruction. Students who are retained tend to have lower academic achievement than those who are promoted, and drop out of school at higher rates (National Research Council, 1999a).

Placing high-stakes accountability on students also poses special problems. For one thing, tests that are used to make decisions about schools may be ill-suited for decisions about individual students. In addition, states and districts face substantial legal hurdles in using tests to apply consequences to students. Specifically, they need to demonstrate that the tests neither discriminate against any group of students nor deny any student due process. To demonstrate the latter, states need to prove that students have received adequate notice of high-stakes testing requirements and that they have been taught the knowledge and skills the test measures (*Debra P. v. Turlington*, 1981).

For these and other reasons, the Committee on Appropriate Test Use of the National Research Council (National Research Council, 1999a:279) recommended that "high-stakes decisions [about individual students] such as tracking, promotion, and graduation should not automatically be made on the basis of a single test but should be buttressed by other relevant information about the student's knowledge and skills, such as grades, teacher recommendations, and extenuating circumstances."

Accountability for What? Determining what students or schools should be held accountable for is no less challenging than determining whom to hold accountable. The Title I statute and the new accountability ideas it reflects hold that the answer is "student performance." But in practice, this answer leads to a number of interpretations, and the way schools respond to those interpretations affects whether accountability realizes its goals of increasing learning for all students.

As noted above, one of the major purposes of accountability based on performance is to encourage schools to focus their efforts on improving performance above all else. Everyone held accountable has an incentive to ensure that performance increases—or at least to stave off declines.

In the past, though, efforts to raise stakes on tests have not always had the desired effect. In some cases, schools employed inappropriate practices to raise test scores, such as focusing instruction on the format or general content of tests, rather than the concepts and skills the tests were expected to measure. These practices may have boosted scores, at least temporarily, but they did not in fact raise achievement (Koretz et al., 1991). Occasionally, schools resorted to practices that were unethical or illegal, including cheating.

The phenomenon of raising test scores without raising achievement occurs only under certain circumstances, although these circumstances happen to be relatively common. The first is when schools use tests that are not particularly sensitive to instruction. Tests that measure general knowledge and skills, rather than the knowledge and skills schools are focusing on, do not respond immediately to instructional changes, no matter how effective. So in order to raise scores quickly, schools employ test-based strategies, and achievement does not increase. If, however, schools used instructionally sensitive instruction, they could raise scores and achievement by improving instruction.

Another factor that contributes to inappropriate test preparation strategies is the use of a single test as the basis for rewards and sanctions. Although the Title I statute calls for the use of multiple measures of student achievement, states and districts at this point continue to use one test in designing accountability. Schools get the message that they have to raise scores on that test in order to earn rewards or avoid sanctions. Using multiple measures could encourage schools to focus less on a single measure and more on improving achievement generally.

In an effort to broaden the measure of achievement, some states include additional factors for accountability. Texas, for example, includes graduation rates and attendance rates, along with test scores, in determining ratings for schools. But few schools have earned low ratings because of these factors; as a result, schools continue to focus their attention on the tests (Gordon and Reese, 1997).

The way that states calculate performance also affects schools' responses to accountability. In some states, schools or districts must reach a threshold level of performance in order to earn rewards; that is, a certain percentage of students must attain a passing score or reach a particular level of proficiency. In these states, some schools reason that the most efficient way of meeting those targets is to focus on students who are just below the bar, and provide them with intensive test preparation.

As Willms (1998) found, this strategy may be shortsighted. Examining data from British Columbia, he found that schools that improved performance overall did so by raising the performance of low-performing students. This occurred, he notes, because high-performing students tend to do well in any circumstances; raising the floor also raises overall performance.

Other states have tried to encourage schools to focus their efforts on low-performing students by placing an emphasis on improving the distribution of performance, and reducing the number of low performers as well as increasing the average. In these states, test preparation for a few students will not work; improving instruction across the board will earn them rewards.

Test preparation alone will also be effective only if the objective is to reach a certain level of performance, rather than to improve performance continually. States such as Kentucky, where schools must reach new performance goals every two years, have found that they can raise performance in the early years by focusing on the test; sustaining gains requires instructional improvement—which in turn requires support for professional development.

Rewards and Sanctions. Taking a leaf from the business and organizational literature, designers of accountability mechanisms have sought to create tangible rewards for high performance and significant penalties for poor performance. The goal was to create real incentives for change, rather than relying simply on the good will and best efforts of teachers and administrators.

The practices have varied widely. Nearly all states, and many districts, have simply published performance results, or provided them to newspapers, which published them. By making the information public, officials reasoned, schools would have an incentive to improve to look their best in the media and have an answer for parents and public officials who questioned their performance. These public reporting systems certainly attracted the public's attention; whether they produced any real change is not clear (Elmore et al., 1996).

In other cases, states and districts have tried more stringent methods to spur change. Some 14 states offer rewards to high-performing schools (Education Week, 1998). These include ceremonial honors, such as blue ribbons, as well as cash awards. South Carolina and Mississippi relaxed certain state regulations for schools that performed above a designated level.

The power of these rewards as motivations for change is unclear. In Kentucky, where the state provided cash bonuses to schools amounting to between $1,300 and $2,600 per certified staff member, the bonuses did not appear to have much effect (Elmore et al., 1996). Some teachers doubted whether the bonuses would in fact materialize, citing a previously announced bonus plan that died aborning. Whatever the reason, teachers did not appear to pay much attention to the prospect of cash awards.

More significant in Kentucky, and elsewhere, was the threat of sanctions (Kelley et al., 1998). Some 31 states provide some sort of penalty for failing schools (Education Week, 1998), ranging from requiring a state-approved improvement plan, to reconstitution (replacing the entire faculty and staff), to state takeover. Few states have actually imposed the most dramatic sanctions; the threats themselves appear to have spurred schools into action. The threats have even attracted the notice of schools that are not at risk of intervention (Firestone et al., 1998).

Many states and districts that have not imposed sanctions have offered assistance to troubled schools. Assistance can take the form of technical help in writing school improvement plans, as in Mississippi, or a state-appointed monitoring team that oversees the implementation of a reform plan, as in New York State. These assistance efforts have helped to turn troubled schools around; however, it is not clear whether states or districts have sufficient capacity to assist all schools that need help. A survey by the U.S. Department of Education found that only 9 states report that they can provide support to at least half the schools in need of improvement; 12 states report that they serve less than half of schools in need of improvement; and 24 states say they have more schools in need of improvement than they can serve (U.S. Department of Education,

1999). Even if states that can provide assistance to the lowest-performing schools, few serve schools in the middle of the performance distribution, which tend to receive less attention from the state accountability efforts (Massell, 1998).

The ability of accountability mechanisms to produce desired effects depends on the level of *internal* accountability within schools (Abelmann and Elmore, 1999). That is, teachers' own judgments about their ability to affect the learning of their students governs the teachers' willingness to take responsibility for improving student learning and to change their practice to make such improvements come about. Misalignment between internal and external accountability may make it less likely that external systems, no matter how strong, will have much effect.

Internal accountability includes the norms by which teachers operate, the expectations they hold about student learning and their role in improving it, and the processes they use to carry out their work. In schools with weak internal accountability, the norms emphasize the individual responsibility of each teacher over student learning, rather than the collective responsibility of the entire school. In those cases, teachers' judgments about whether and how much they could improve learning depend on their understanding of the students' background and lack a perspective of what students could do under different circumstances.

Similarly, the expectations for student learning in such schools are relatively low, since teachers believe that the conditions the students brought to school, rather than their own efforts, exert the greatest influence over their academic performance. Teachers in schools with low internal accountability tend to place a greater emphasis on order, an expectation each teacher shares.

Schools with weak internal accountability therefore tend to respond to external pressures for change by summoning their own individual beliefs, rather than by consulting with colleagues and attempting to work collectively for improvement.

ecommendations

- Accountability should follow responsibility: teachers and administrators—individually and collectively—should be held accountable for their part in improving student performance. Teachers and administrators should be accountable for the progress of their students. Districts and states should be accountable for the professional development and support they provide teachers and schools to enable students to reach high standards.
- Accountability decisions should be based on multiple indicators.
- Accountability mechanisms should be based on a range of measures, including indicators of instructional quality, as well as student outcomes.

• Accountability results should be reported so that the improvements needed are clear to students, teachers, and parents.

• Accountability mechanisms should encourage schools to improve all students' performance.

• Assistance should be aimed at strengthening schools' capacity for educating all students to high standards and to building the internal accountability within schools.

Questions to Ask

❑ Are teachers and administrators held accountable for the progress of their students, and are districts and the state held accountable for the professional development and support they provide teachers and schools to enable students to reach high standards?

❑ Are multiple indicators used in determining accountability, including indicators of instructional quality, as well as student outcomes?

❑ Are accountability results reported so that the improvements needed are clear to students, teachers, and parents?

❑ Does the accountability mechanism encourage schools to improve all students' performance?

❑ Does your accountability system provide assistance to build capacity and internal accountability in schools?

Criteria

Link to Instructional Improvement. The accountability system should be tied directly to the instructional improvement system, so that all schools can learn from the example of the successful schools and poor-performing schools can receive the support they need to improve.

Assistance Before Sanctions. Penalties such as reconstitution and takeovers are not solutions; they are means to implement solutions. State and district efforts should emphasize assistance first, and sanctions only after a period of continual decline in performance and evidence that additional help would be fruitless.

Assistance to All, with Priority for Lowest-Performing Schools. The poorest-performing schools would benefit most from assistance and should receive it first, but all schools need some form of help in developing teacher capacity and internal accountability.

*E*xamples

The following examples come from two states that have shown the largest gains in performance on the National Assessment of Educational Progress— North Carolina and Texas. In each state, accountability has created incentives for improvement. North Carolina's system links accountability directly to improvement for low-performing schools; Texas's system encourages schools to direct their efforts at improving education for all students.

Under North Carolina's accountability system, known as the ABCs of Public Education, the state measures student performance on the state assessment and creates an "expected growth" composite for each school based on statewide average growth and the previous performance of students in the school. The state then adjusts the results statistically to compare student performance from one year to the next.

Schools are designated as "low-performing" if less than 50 percent of their students achieve standards, which is defined as at or above grade level in reading, mathematics, and writing. Low-performing schools are assigned assistance teams of educators who work with school staffs to align the curriculum to state standards.

The state also recognizes schools that have large percentages of high-performing students, or that demonstrate large gains in perfor- mance. Schools that meet their expected growth standard and have at least 90 percent of students performing at or above grade level (in K-8) or at above Achievement Level III (in high school) are designated as Schools of Excellence and are recognized at a state luncheon and receive cash awards. Schools with 80 percent of students at or above grade level of Achievement Level III are designated Schools of Distinction. Schools that show exemplary gains—10 percent or more above the statewide average—receive cash awards; the 25 schools that gained the greatest amount are honored at a statewide luncheon. Schools must test at least 95 percent of the student body (98 percent in K-8 schools) in order to be eligible for recognition.

In Texas, students and teachers know that the TAAS (the Texas Assessment of Academic Skills) matters. The tests play a central role in the state accountability system, for students and institutions. Under state law, students must pass each section of the exit-level exam in order to graduate from high school. Students may retake any part of the test they do not pass; students now can take the test up to eight times. When the full battery of end-of-course exams is implemented, students may be able to graduate by passing these tests, rather than the TAAS.

The tests matter to schools and districts, too, because they are judged in large part on their ability to enable students to pass the test. The state has developed an elaborate accountability rating system that classifies schools and districts by using their TAAS passing rates, dropout rates, and attendance rates.

Under the system, the state rates districts each year in four categories: exemplary, recognized, academically acceptable, and academically unacceptable. The state also rates schools in the following categories: exemplary, recognized, acceptable, and low-performing. The standards for each designation have risen over the past few years, as performance has improved.

Significantly, schools must demonstrate that students in each group—black, Hispanic, white, and economically disadvantaged—as well as students overall, have met the required passing rates in order to earn a status of acceptable or above. In this way, schools cannot attain high ratings if only a small group of their students perform well.

Schools rated as acceptable or low-performing or districts rated academically acceptable or academically unacceptable must show required improvement. To meet that standard, a school or district with a TAAS passing rate below 40 percent in any area must show that, over two years, its rate of change exceeded the rate required to reach a 50 percent passing level within five years. A school or district with a dropout rate above 6 percent must show a two-year rate of change that would meet or exceed the rate needed to reach a 6 percent rate within five years.

The accreditation ratings are used to determine rewards and sanctions. High-performing schools, those designated exemplary or recognized, and those designated acceptable that have demonstrated significant gains in student performance, are eligible to share monetary awards. In 1997-1998, the legislature appropriated a total of $5 million over two years for such financial awards; schools can receive between $500 and $5,000. These financial awards are not considered a significant motivation to improve performance.

The sanctions are considered more important. For districts that are academically unacceptable, the state commissioner may order the district to publish the ratings to all property owners and parents; require the district to develop an improvement plan; appoint a master to oversee the operations of the district or a management team to direct operations in low-performing areas. If districts are rated academically unacceptable for a year or more, the state may replace the school board; if a district is rated academically unacceptable for two years or more, the state may annex the district to a neighboring district.

For schools that are designated low-performing, the state may notify the district of its status; require the school to develop an improvement plan; or appoint a special intervention team to conduct an on-site evaluation and recommend appropriate changes in budget, personnel, or school policies. If a school is designated low-performing for a year or more, the state may appoint a board of managers to assume the school board's authority over the school. A school designated low-performing for two years or more may be shut down.

Perhaps the most important spur to improvement is the simple publication of results. Not only are accountability ratings made available to the media, but the results are publicly available on the state's Internet home page. In addition, all schools are required to send school report cards to parents. These report cards must include state-generated data related to the accountability system. The public awareness of the results and the accountability ratings that these reports generate play a significant role for school leaders.

References

Abedi, Jamal

    1995   *Language Background as a Variable in NAEP Mathematics Performance.* Los Angeles: Center for Research on Evaluation, Standards, and Student Testing, University of California, Los Angeles.

Abelmann, Charles, and Richard F. Elmore with J. Even, S. Kenyon, and J. Marshall

    1999   *When Accountability Knocks, Will Anyone Answer?* CPRE Research Report No. RR-042. Philadelphia: University of Pennsylvania, Consortium for Policy Research in Education.

Advisory Commission on Testing in Chapter 1

    1993   *Reinforcing the Promise, Reforming the Paradigm: Report of the Advisory Commission on Testing in Chapter 1.* Washington, DC: U.S. Department of Education.

American Educational Research Association, American Psychological Association, and National Council on Measurement in Education

    1985   *Standards for Educational and Psychological Tests.* Washington, DC: American Psychological Association.

    In   *Standards for Educational and Psychological Tests.* Washington, DC: American
    Press Psychological Association.

American Federation of Teachers

    1998   *Making Standards Matter.* Washington, DC: American Federation of Teachers.

Aschbacher, Pamela R.

    1994   Helping educators to develop and use alternative assessments: Barriers and facilitators. *Educational Policy* 8(2):202-223.

Baker, E.L.

    1997   Model-based performance assessment. *Theory Into Practice* 36(4):247-254.

Baker, Eva L., and Robert L. Linn

    1997   *Emerging Educational Standards of Performance in the United States.* CSE Technical Report 437. Los Angeles: University of California, National Center for Research on Evaluation, Standards, and Student Testing.

Baker, Eva L., M. Freeman, and S. Clayton

1991   Cognitive assessment of history for large-scale testing. Pp. 131-153 in *Testing and Cognition*, M.C. Wittrock and E.L. Baker, eds. Englewood Cliffs, NJ: Prentice-Hall.

Baker, E.L, D. Niemi, H. Herl, A. Aguirre-Muñoz, L. Staley, and R.L. Linn

1999   *Report on the Content Area Performance Assessments (CAPA): A Collaboration Among the Hawaii Department of Education, the Center for Research on Evaluation, Standards, and Student Testing (CRESST) and the Teachers and Children of Hawaii* (Final Deliverable). Los Angeles: University of California, National Center for Research on Evaluation, Standards, and Student Testing.

Bishop, John H.

1994   *The Payoff to Schooling and Learning in the United States.* Ithaca, NY: School of Industrial and Labor Relations, Cornell University.

Bridgeman, Brent, Edward Chittenden, and Frederick Cline

1995   *Characteristics of a Portfolio Scale for Rating Early Literacy.* Princeton, NJ: Center for Performance Assessment, Educational Testing Service.

Calfee, Robert, and W.V. Masuda

1997   Classroom assessment as inquiry. Pp. 69-102 in *Handbook of Classroom Assessment.* G. Phye, ed. San Diego: Academic Press.

Carlson, Dale C.

1996   Adequate Yearly Progress in Title I of the Improving America's Schools Act of 1994: Issues and Strategies. Washington, DC: State Collaborative on Assessment of Student Standards, Council of Chief State School Officers.

Chun, Tammi J., and Margaret E. Goertz

1999   Title I and state education policy: High standards for all students? in *Hard Work for Good Schools: Facts Not Fads in Title I Reform.* Gary Orfield and Elizabeth H. DeBray, eds. Cambridge, MA: The Civil Rights Project, Harvard University.

Citizens' Commission on Civil Rights

1998   *Title I at Midstream: The Fight to Improve Schools for Poor Kids.* Corrine M. Yu and William L. Taylor, eds. Washington, DC: Citizens' Commission on Civil Rights.

Clotfelter, Charles T., and Helen F. Ladd

1996   Recognizing and rewarding success in public schools. Pp. 23-64 in *Holding Schools Accountable.* Helen C. Ladd, ed. Washington, DC: Brookings Institution, 23-64.

Cohen, David K., and Heather Hill

1998   *Instructional Policy and Classroom Performance: The Mathematics Reform in California.* Ann Arbor: University of Michigan.

Council for Basic Education

1998   *Great Expectations?* Scott Joftus and Ilene Berman. Washington, DC: Council for Basic Education.

Council of Chief State School Officers

1998   *Trends in State Student Assessment Programs, Fall 1997.* Linda Bond, Edward D. Roeber. Washington, D.C.: Council of Chief State School Officers.

Cronbach, Lee J., Norman M. Bradburn, and D.G. Horvitz

1994   *Sampling and Statistical Procedures Used in the California Learning Assessment System.* Report of the Select Committee. Stanford, CA: Stanford University.

David, Jane M.

   1997   The Role of Standards-Based Assessment in Schoolwide Instructional Improvement: Necessary, Perhaps, But Not Sufficient. Paper prepared for the New Standards Evaluation Steering Committee.

Education Week

   1998   *Quality Counts, 1998.* Washington, DC: Editorial Projects in Education Inc.

Elmore, Richard F.

   1996   Getting to scale with good educational practice. *Harvard Educational Review* 66(1):1-26.

   1997   *Investing in Teacher Learning: Staff Development and Instructional Improvement in Community District #2, New York City.* New York: National Commission on Teaching and America's Future.

Elmore, Richard F., Charles H. Abelmann, and Susan H. Fuhrman

   1996   The new accountability in state education reform: From process to performance. Pp 65-98 in *Holding Schools Accountable.* Helen C. Ladd, ed. Washington, DC: Brookings Institution.

Elmore, Richard F., and Deanna Burney

   1998   *The Challenge of School Variability: Improving Instruction in New York City's Community District #2.* Philadelphia: Center for Policy Research in Education, University of Pennsylvania.

Finn, Chester E., Jr., Marci Kanstoroom, and Michael J. Petrelli

   1999   Overview: Thirty years of dashed hopes. In *New Directions: Federal Education Policy in the Twenty-First Century.* Marci Kanstoroom and Chester E. Finn, Jr., eds. Washington, DC: Thomas B. Fordham Foundation.

Firestone, William A., David Mayrowitz, and Janet Fairman

   1998   Performance-based assessment and instructional change: The effects of testing in Maine and Maryland. *Educational Evaluation and Policy Analysis.* 20(2):95-113.

Fordham Foundation

   1998   *The State of State Standards.* Chester E. Finn, Jr., Michael J. Petrelli, and Gregg Vanourek. Washington, DC: Thomas B. Fordham Foundation.

Fullan, Michael, with S. Stiegelbauer

   1991   *The New Meaning of Educational Change.* New York: Teachers College Press.

Glaser, Robert

   1991   Expertise and assessment. Pp. 17-30 in *Testing and Cognition.* M.C. Wittrock and E.L. Baker, eds. Englewood Cliffs, NJ: Prentice-Hall.

Gordon, Stephen P., and Marianne Reese

   1997   High stakes testing: Worth the price? *Journal of School Leadership* 7 (July).

Graue, M. Elizabeth

   1999   Assessment in Early Childhood Education. Paper prepared for the Committee on Title I Testing and Assessment, National Research Council.

Grissmer, David, and Ann Flanagan

   1998   *Exploring Rapid Achievement Gains in North Carolina and Texas.* Washington, DC: National Education Goals Panel.

Hambleton, Ronald K.

   1998   Setting performance standards on achievement tests: Meeting the requirements of Title I. In *Handbook for the Development of Performance Standards: Meeting the Requirements of Title I.* Linda N. Hansche, ed. Prepared for the U.S. Department of Education and the Council of Chief State School Officers. Washington, DC: U.S. Department of Education and the Council of Chief State School Officers.

Hansche, Linda N.
   1998 *Handbook for the Development of Performance Standards: Meeting the Requirements of Title I.* Prepared for the U.S. Department of Education and the Council of Chief State School Officers. Washington, DC: U.S. Department of Education and the Council of Chief State School Officers.

Independent Review Panel
   1999 *Measured Progress: The Report of the Independent Review Panel on the Evaluation of Federal Education Legislation.* Washington, DC: U.S. Department of Education.

Jaeger, Richard M., and Charlene G. Tucker
   1998 *Analyzing, Disaggregating, Reporting, and Interpreting Students' Achievement Test Results: A Guide to Practice for Title I and Beyond.* Washington, DC: Council of Chief State School Officers.

Kelley, Carolyn, A. Milanowski, and H.G. Heneman III
   1998 Changing Teacher Compensation: Cross-Site Analysis of the Effects of School-Based Peformance Award Programs. Paper presented at the Annual Meeting of the American Educational Research Association, San Diego, April.

Koretz, Daniel M.
   1997 *The Assessment of Students With Disabilities in Kentucky.* Los Angeles: Center for Research on Evaluation, Standards, and Student Testing, University of California, Los Angeles.

Koretz, Daniel M., Sheila Barron, Karen J. Mitchell, and Brian M. Stecher
   1996 *Perceived Effects of the Kentucky Instructional Results Information System (KIRIS).* Santa Monica, CA: RAND.

Koretz, Daniel M., Robert L. Linn, Stephen B. Dunbar, and Lorrie A. Shepard
   1991 The Effects of High-Stakes Testing on Achievement: Preliminary Findings About Generalization Across Tests. Paper presented at the Annual Meeting of the American Educational Research Association, Chicago, April 5.

Koretz, Daniel, Daniel McCaffery, Stephen Klein, Robert Bell, and Brian Stecher
   1993 *The Reliability of Scores From the 1992 Vermont Portfolio Assessment Program.* Los Angeles: Center for Research on Evaluation, Standards, and Student Testing, University of California, Los Angeles.

Marzano, Robert J., John S. Kendall, and Barbara B. Gaddy
   1999 *Essential Knowledge: The Debate Over What American Students Should Know.* Aurora, CO: Mid-Continent Regional Education Laboratory.

Massell, Diane
   1998 *State Strategies for Building Capacity in Education.* Philadelphia: Consortium for Policy Research in Education, University of Pennsylvania.

Massell, Diane, Michael W. Kirst, and M. Hoppe
   1997 *Persistence and Change: Standards-Based Reform in Nine States.* CPRE Research Report No. RR-037. Philadelphia: University of Pennsylvania, Consortium for Policy Research in Education.

McLaughlin, Milbrey W., and Lorrie A. Shepard
   1995 *Improving Education Through Standards-Based Reform.* A report of the National Academy of Education Panel on Standards-Based Reform. Stanford, CA: National Academy of Education.

Meisels, Samuel J.

1996   Performance in context: Assessing children's achievement at the outset of school. Pp. 410-431 in *The Five to Seven Year Shift: The Age of Reason and Responsibility.* A.J. Sameroff and M.M. Haith, eds. Chicago: University of Chicago Press.

Mills, Craig N., and Richard M. Jaeger

1998   Creating descriptions of desired student achievement when setting performance standards. In *Handbook for the Development of Performance Standards: Meeting the Requirements of Title I.* Linda N. Hansche, ed. Prepared for the U.S. Department of Education and the Council of Chief State School Officers. Washington, DC: U.S. Department of Education and the Council of Chief State School Officers.

Mislevy, Robert

1993   Foundations of a new test theory. Pp. 19-40 in *Test Theory for a New Generation of Tests.* N. Frederiksen, R.J. Mislevey, and I.I. Bejar, eds. Hillsdale, NJ: Erlbaum.

National Center for Education Statistics

1999   *Teacher Quality: A Report on the Preparation and Qualifications of Public School Teachers.* NCES 1999-080. Laurie Lewis, Basmat Parsad, Nancy Carey, Nicole Bartfai, Elizabeth Farris, and Becky Smerdon. Washington, DC: National Center for Education Statistics.

National Center on Education and the Economy and the University of Pittsburgh

1997   *Performance Standards: Volume 1-Elementary School.* Washington, DC: National Center on Education and the Economy and the University of Pittsburgh.

National Education Goals Panel

1993   *Promises to Keep: Creating High Standards for American Students.* Washington, DC: National Education Goals Panel.

National Governors' Association

1986   *Time for Results.* Washington, DC: National Governors' Association.

National Partnership for Excellence and Accountability in Teaching

1999   Principles of Effective Professional Development. www.npeat.org. Washington, DC: National Partnership for Excellence and Accountability in Teaching.

National Research Council

1996   *National Science Education Standards.* National Committee on Science Education Standards and Assessments. Washington, DC: National Academy Press.

1997a *Educating One and All.* Lorraine M. McDonnell, Margaret J. McLaughlin, and Patricia Morison, eds. Committee on Goals 2000 and the Inclusion of Students with Disabilities. Washington, DC: National Academy Press.

1997b *Improving Schooling for Language Minority Children.* Kenji Hakuta and Diane August, eds. Committee on Developing a Research Agenda on the Education of Limited English Proficient and Bilingual Students. Washington, DC: National Academy Press.

1998   *Grading the Nation's Report Card: Evaluating NAEP and Transforming the Assessment of Educational Progress.* James W. Pelligrino, Lee R. Jones, and Karen J. Mitchell, eds. Committee on the Evaluation of National and State Assessments of Educational Progress. Washington, DC: National Academy Press.

1999a *High Stakes: Testing for Tracking, Promotion, and Graduation.* Jay P. Heubert and Robert M. Hauser, eds. Committee on Appropriate Test Use. Washington, DC: National Academy Press.

1999b *Uncommon Measures: Equivalence and Linking Among Educational Tests.* Michael J. Feuer, Paul W. Holland, Bert F. Green, Meryl W. Bertenthal, and F. Cadelle Hemphill, eds. Committee on Equivalency and Linkage of Educational Tests. Washington, DC: National Academy Press.

Natriello, Gary, and Edward L. McDill

1999 Title I: From funding mechanism to educational program. In *Hard Work for Good Schools: Facts Not Fads in Title I Reform.* Gary Orfield and Elizabeth H. DeBray, eds. Cambridge, MA: The Civil Rights Project, Harvard University.

Newmann, Fred M., and Associates

1996 *Authentic Achievement: Restructuring Schools for Intellectual Quality.* San Francisco: Jossey-Bass Publishers Inc.

Newmann, Fred M., Gudelia Lopez, and Anthony S. Bryk

1998 *The Quality of Intellectual Work in Chicago Schools: A Baseline Report.* Chicago: Consortium on Chicago School Research.

Niemi, David

1997 Cognitive science, expert-novice research, and performance assessment. *Theory Into Practice* 36(4):239-246.

O'Day, Jennifer

In *Reconstitution as a Remedy for School Failure.* CPRE Policy Brief. Philadelphia:
Press University of Pennsylvania, Consortium for Policy Research in Education.

Office of Technology Assessment

1992 *Testing in American Schools: Asking the Right Questions.* Washington, DC: U.S. Government Printing Office.

Orfield, Gary

1999 Strengthening Title I: Designing a policy based on evidence. In *Hard Work for Good Schools: Facts Not Fads in Title I Reform.* Gary Orfield and Elizabeth H. DeBray, eds. Cambridge, MA: The Civil Rights Project, Harvard University.

Osborne, David, and Ted Gaebler

1993 *Reinventing Government. How the Entrepreneurial Spirit is Transforming the Public Sector.* New York: Plume/Penguin Books.

Picus, Lawrence O., and Alisha Tralli

1998 *Alternative Assessment Programs; What Are the True Costs? An Analysis of Total Costs of Assessment in Kentucky and Vermont.* CSE Technical Report 441. Los Angeles, CA: National Center for Research on Evaluation, Standards and Student Testing, University of California, Los Angeles.

Plake, Barbara S., and James C. Impara

1997 Teacher assessment literacy: What do teachers know about assessment. Pp. 53-68 in *Handbook of Classroom Assessment.* G. Phye, ed. San Diego: Academic Press.

Puma, Michael J., Nancy Karweit, Cristofer Price, Anne Ricciuti, William Thompson, and Michael Vaden-Kiernan

1997 *Prospects: Final Report on Student Outcomes.* Cambridge, MA: Abt Associates Inc.

Ragland, Mary A., Rose Asera, and Joseph F. Johnson, Jr.

1999 *Urgency, Responsibility, Efficacy: Preliminary Findings of a Study of High-Performing Texas School Districts.* Austin, TX: Charles A. Dana Center, University of Texas at Austin.

Ragosa, David R.

    1994   *Misclassification in Student Performance Categories. Appendix to CLAS Technical Report.* Monterey, CA: CTB/McGraw-Hill.

Raudenbush, Stephen W., and J. Douglas Willms

    1995   The estimation of school effects. *Journal of Educational and Behavioral Statistics* 20(4):307-335.

Ravitch, Diane

    1995   *National Standards in American Education: A Citizen's Guide.* Washington, DC: The Brookings Institution.

    1999   Student performance: The national agenda in education. In *New Directions: Federal Education Policy in the Twenty-First Century.* Marci Kanstoroom and Chester E. Finn, Jr., eds. Washington, DC: Thomas B. Fordham Foundation.

Resnick, Lauren B., and Daniel P. Resnick

    1992   Assessing the thinking curriculum: New tools for educational reform. In *Changing Assessments: Alternative Views of Aptitude, Achievement, and Instruction.* B.R. Gifford and M.C. O'Connor, eds. Boston: Kluwer Academic Publishing.

Sanders, W.L., and S.P. Horn

    1995   The Tennessee Value-Added Assessment System (TVAAS): Mixed-model methodology in educational assessment. Pp. 337-350 in *Teacher Evaluation: Guide to Effective Practice.* A.J. Shinkfield and D. Stufflebeam, eds. Boston: Kluwer Academic Publishing.

Schmidt, William H., Curtis C. McKnight, Pamela M. Jakwerth, Leland S. Cogan, Senta A. Raizen, Richard T. Houang, Gilbert A. Valverde, David E. Wiley, Richard G. Wolfe, Leonard G. Bianchi, Wen-Ling Yang, Seung-Ho Kang, and Edward D. Britton

    1998   *Facing the Consequences: Using TIMSS for a Closer Look at United States Mathematics and Science Education.* Boston: Kluwer Academic Publishing.

Shavelson, Richard J., X. Gao, and Gail P. Baxter

    1993   *Sampling Variability of Performance Assessments.* Los Angeles: Center for Research on Evaluation, Standards, and Student Testing, University of California, Los Angeles.

Shepard, Lorrie A.

    1989   Inflated Test Score Gains: Is it Old Norms or Teaching to the Test? Paper presented at the Annual Meeting of the American Educational Research Association, San Francisco, March.

    1991   Will national tests improve student learning? *Phi Delta Kappan* 73(3):232-239.

    1994   The challenges of assessing young children appropriately. *Phi Delta Kappan* November:206-212.

Shepard, Lorrie A., Sharon L. Kagan, and Emily C. Wurtz

    1998a   *Principles and Recommendations for Early Childhood Assessments.* Washington, DC: National Education Goals Panel.

Shepard, Lorrie A., G. Taylor, and D. Betebenner

    1998b   *Infusion of Limited-English-Proficient Students in Rhode Island's Grade 4 Mathematics Performance Assessment.* Los Angeles, CA: Center for Research on Evaluation, Standards, and Student Testing, University of California, Los Angeles.

Smith, Julia B., BetsAnn Smith, and Anthony S. Bryk

    1998   *Setting the Pace: Opportunities to Learn in Chicago's Elementary Schools.* Chicago: Consortium on Chicago School Research.

Smith, S.W.

   1990   Individualized education programs (IEPs) in special education: From intent to acquiescence. *Exceptional Children* 57(1): 6-14.

Spillane, James P.

   1997   External Reform Initiatives and Teachers' Efforts to Reconstruct Their Practice: The Mediating Role of Teachers' Zones of Enactment. Paper presented at the Annual Meeting of the Association for Public Policy Analysis and Management, Washington, DC, November.

Stecher, Brian M., Sheila Barron, Tessa Kaganoff, and Joy Goodwin

   1998   *The Effects of Standards-Based Assessment on Classroom Practices: Results of the 1996-97 RAND Survey of Kentucky Teachers of Mathematics and Writing.* Los Angeles: Center for Research on Evaluation, Standards, and Student Testing, University of California, Los Angeles.

Teachers of English to Speakers of Other Languages, Inc.

   1997   *ESL Standards for Pre-K-12 Students..* Bloomington, IL: Pantagraph Printing.

Thurlow, Martha L., Allison L. Seyfarth, Dorene L. Scott, and James E. Ysseldyke

   1997   State Assessment Policies on Participation and Accommodations for Students with Disabilities: 1997 Update. Minneapolis: National Center on Educational Outcomes, University of Minnesota.

U.S. Department of Education

   1999   *Promising Results, Continuing Challenges: The Final Report of the National Assessment of Title I.* Washington, DC: U.S. Department of Education.

Wang, Margaret C., Kenneth K. Wong, and Jeong-Ran Kim

   1999   The need for developing procedural accountability in Title I schoolwide programs. In *Hard Work for Good Schools: Facts Not Fads in Title I Reform.* Gary Orfield and Elizabeth H. DeBray, eds. Cambridge, MA: The Civil Rights Project, Harvard University.

Webb, Norman

   1997   Criteria for Alignment of Expectations and Assessments in Mathematics and Science Education. Madison: University of Wisconsin-Madison, National Institute for Science Education.

Webb, Norman, and Thomas A. Romberg

   1992   Implications of the NCTM standards for mathematics assessment. Pp. 37–60 in *Mathematics Assessment and Evaluation: Imperatives for Mathematics Educators.* T.A. Romberg, ed. Albany: State University of New York Press.

Western Michigan University Evaluation Center

   1995   *An Independent Evaluation of the Kentucky Instructional Results Information System (KIRIS).* Frankfort: Kentucky Institute for Education Research.

Willms, J. Douglas

   1998   Assessment Strategies for Title I of the Improving America's Schools Act. Paper prepared for the Committee on Title I Testing and Assessment, National Research Council.

Wixson, Karen K., and Elizabeth Dutro

   1998   *Standards for Primary Grade Reading: An Analysis of State Frameworks.* Ann Arbor: Center for the Improvement of Early Reading Achievement, University of Michigan.

Wixson, Karen K., Maria C. Fisk, Elizabeth Dutro, and Julie McDaniel
  1999   The Alignment of State Standards and Assessments in Elementary Reading. Paper prepared for the Committee on Title I Testing and Assessment, National Research Council.
Yoon, Bokhee, and Lauren B. Resnick
  1998   *Instructional Validity, Opportunity to Learn, and Equity: New Standards Examinations for the California Mathematics Renaissance.* Los Angeles: Center for Research on Evaluation, Standards, and Student Testing, University of California, Los Angeles.
Young, Michael J., and Bokhee Yoon
  1998   *Estimating the Consistency and Accuracy of Classifications in a Standards-Referenced Assessment.* Los Angeles: Center for Research on Evaluation, Standards, and Student Testing, University of California, Los Angeles.

Biographical Sketches

Richard F. Elmore (Chair) is professor of education and the chairman of the Department of Administration, Planning and Social Policy at the Graduate School of Education at Harvard University. He is also a senior research fellow of the Consortium for Policy Research in Education. His research focuses on state-local relations in educational policy, school organization, and educational choice. He was a member of the NRC's Commission on Behavioral and Social Sciences and Education, and was a member of the NRC's Board on Testing and Assessment from 1993 to 1997. He has a Ph.D. in educational policy from Harvard University (1976).

Eva L. Baker is professor in the Divisions of Psychological Studies in Education and Social Research Methodologies and the acting dean of the Graduate School of Education and Information Studies at the University of California, Los Angeles. She also is the co-director of the Center for Research on Evaluation, Standards and Student Testing. Her research focuses on the integration of teaching and measurement, including the design of instructional systems and new measures of complex human performances. She served on the NRC Panel on Data Confidentiality and the NAS Panel on Education Reform. She has an Ed.D. from the University of California, Los Angeles (1967).

Ruben A. Carriedo directs the planning, assessment, and accountability activities in the San Diego Unified School District. He also has served on advisory panels and as a consultant for numerous school-reform initiatives. He has an Ed.D. from the Harvard University Graduate School of Education.

Ursula Casanova is associate professor of educational leadership and policy studies in the College of Education at Arizona State University. Her research focuses on the interface between education and culture, particularly with respect to Hispanic populations, and she is the author of numerous books and articles on putting research into practice. She has a Ph.D. in social and philosophical foundations of education from Arizona State University (1985).

Roberta J. Flexer is associate professor of mathematics education in the Department of Education at the University of Colorado at Boulder. Her research focuses on the teaching and learning of elementary mathematics and on mathematics assessment. She has a Ph.D. in mathematics education from the University of Colorado at Boulder (1973).

Ellen C. Guiney is the executive director of the Boston Plan for Excellence in the Public Schools, a local fund that supports education reform in the Boston Public Schools. Previously, she served as the staff director of the education office of the U.S. Senate Committee on Labor and Human Resources, at the time of the passage of the Improving America's Schools Act. She has an M.A. in English from Boston College.

Kati P. Haycock is the director of The Education Trust in Washington, D.C., a national organization that works with states and districts to improve education in schools and colleges, particularly those serving low-income and minority students. She has worked as an advocate for children and youth and has written widely on raising the achievement of minority and low-income students. She has an M.A. in education policy from the University of California, Berkeley (1983).

Joseph F. Johnson, Jr., is the director of the Collaborative for School Improvement at the Charles A. Dana Center at the University of Texas at Austin. He provides technical assistance to the state education agency and local districts on the use of federal resources for excellence and equity. Previously, he served as the senior director of the Division of Accelerated Instruction at the Texas Education Agency, which administers Title I and other programs. He has a Ph.D. in education administration from the University of Texas at Austin (1992).

Sharon Lynn Kagan is a senior associate at the Bush Center in Child Development and Social Policy at Yale University and a senior research scientist at the Yale Child Study Center. She also is the president of the National Association for the Education of Young Children. Her research interests include the application of child- and parent-development research on public policy. She has an Ed.D. in curriculum and teaching from Columbia University, Teachers College (1979).

Fayneese Miller is associate professor of education and the director of the Center for the Study of Race and Ethnicity in America at Brown University. Her area of research is in social adaptation and social reasoning skills of minority adolescents. She has a Ph.D. in experimental social psychology from Texas Christian University (1981).

Jessie Montano is the director of the Division of Learner Options for the Minnesota Department of Children, Families and Learning. She is responsible for overseeing federal and state grant programs, including Title I, that support student learning and choice. She also serves as a member of the independent review panel for Title I evaluation. She has an M.A. in educational administration from Arizona State University.

P. David Pearson is the John A. Hannah distinguished professor of education in the College of Education at Michigan State University. He is the co-director of the Center for the Improvement of Early Reading Achievement, and in that role he carries out a program of research on reading instruction and assessment. He has served as a member of three NRC committees. He has a Ph.D. in education from the University of Minnesota (1969).

Stephen W. Raudenbush is professor of research design and statistics at the School of Education and senior research scientist at the Institute for Social Research, University of Michigan. His research interests include design and analysis in longitudinal and multilevel research in education. He has an Ed.D. in policy analysis and evaluation research from Harvard University (1984).

Lauren B. Resnick is a professor of psychology and the director of the Learning Research and Development Center at the University of Pittsburgh. She also is the co-director of New Standards, a national organization that has developed student-performance standards and a related system of performance assessments. Her research focuses on cognition and instruction and the design of policies and practices in school systems that reflect best learning principles. She served on the NRC Commission on Behavioral and Social Sciences and Education from 1983 to 1989, and on the NRC Mathematical Sciences Education Board from 1987 to 1990, as well as on numerous committees on testing and instruction. She has an Ed.D. in research in instruction from Harvard University (1962).

Robert Rothman (Study Director) is a program officer with the Board on Testing and Assessment at the National Research Council. Previously, he was director of special projects for the National Center on Education and the Economy and associate editor of *Education Week*. He is the author of *Measuring Up: Standards, Assessment, and School Reform*. He has a B.A. from Yale University in political science (1980).

Warren Simmons is the director of the Annenberg Institute for School Reform, a national educational research and support organization based at Brown University. Previously, he was executive director of the Philadelphia Education Fund, a nonprofit organization that collaborates with the School District of Philadelphia and local organizations to provide technical assistance and support for school reform. He has worked on numerous national and local school reform initiatives, with a particular focus on improving the education of disadvantaged students. He has a Ph.D. in psychology from Cornell University (1979).

Charlene G. Tucker is the coordinator of the high school student assessment unit for the Connecticut State Department of Education. Previously, she served in the program evaluation unit, where she conducted the evaluations for Title I. She has an Ed.D. from the University of Massachusetts at Amherst (1991).

Index

C

California, 81
Center for Applied Linguistics, 61
Chicago, Illinois, 78-79
Clinton, William, 93
Community District 2 (New York), 49, 76-77, 84
Computerized feedback, 18
Connecticut, 27-29
Content standards, *vii*, 4, 8, 24-32
   administrators, 26
   curriculum issues, 25, 28
   defined, 4, 24, 27, 28
   English-language learners, 61, 62
   fairness, 27
   instructional methods, 24-25, 26
   mathematics, 24, 27, 30-32
   professional development, 82
   recommendations, 26-27
   science, 24, 27-29
   state-level, 1, 10, 24, 25, 26, 27-32, 43
   validity issues, 25-26
Cost and cost-benefit factors, *vi*, 2, 11, 16
   alignment, tests and standards, 45
   Title I, general, 1, 7-8
Council for Basic Education, 25
Council of Chief State School Officers, 61
CRESST, *see* National Center for Research on Evaluation, Standards, and Student Testing
Curriculum and curriculum design, 5, 15, 19, 23, 54-55, 77
   accountability, 17, 92
   alignment, *iv, vii, x,* 2, 15, 17, 20, 26, 43-45, 75
   content standards, 25, 28
   flexibility, 9, 17, 18, 92
   professional development and, 79, 81
   test-taking skills and, 8
   see also Instructional methods

D

Department of Education, *vi*, 61, 96
Disabled students, *see* Students with disabilities
Disaggregating data, 71-73, 78
District-level assessment, *see* School district assessment; *specific districts*

E

Early childhood education (K-3), 4, 14, 21, 24, 39-41, 50-55
   accountability, 50, 51-52
   assessment strategies, 4, 14, 21, 24, 39-41, 50-55, 57
   federal role, 4, 50
   multiple measures, 53, 54
   school district assessment, 79, 81
   special education, 51, 52
   state government role, 50-55
   teachers, 52, 53
   validity issues, 52, 54
Economic factors, *v*
   incentives and penalties, 3, 6, 17, 18, 19, 22, 89, 92, 96-97
   poverty, 10, 23-24, 47, 66, 71, 72, 73, 75, 78, 88
   see also Cost and cost-benefit factors; Funding
Educational Testing Service, 52
Education improvement systems, 3-6, 12, 20-22
   accountability, 6, 12-13, 20, 22
   assessment strategies, 4-5, 12-13, 20, 21
   instructional methods, 3, 4, 5-6, 21, 22
   performance standards, 3, 4, 5, 21
   reporting requirements, 21
   standards, general, 3-6, 20, 21
   state government role, 3, 5, 12, 21
Elementary and Secondary Education Act (Title I), *see* Federal government
Elementary education, 10, 50
   mathematics standards, 36-37
   science standards, 24, 28-29
   Title I students, number of, 1, 7
   yearly progress requirements, 87, 89
   see also Early childhood education
English-language learners, 5, 10, 21, 38-41, 61-66, 72, 73
   accommodations, 61-66 (passim)
   accountability, 63-64, 65
   assessment strategies, 5, 10, 21, 38-41, 61-66
   content standards, 61, 62
   federal government role, 60, 61, 63
   multiple measures, 63, 66
   performance standards, 38-39
   school district role, 62, 63, 64, 65-66
   standards, general, 61-62
   state government role, 61, 62, 63, 64-65
   validity issues, 61, 63, 64
Evaluation, *see* Accountability; Assessment strategies; Standards

N

National Assessment Governing Board, 68
National Assessment of Educational Progress, 68, 99
National Association for Bilingual Education, 61
National Center for Research on Evaluation, Standards, and Student Testing, 45, 70
National Council of Teachers of Mathematics Standards, 15, 24
National Educational Goals Panel, 18, 33, 51
National Governor's Association, 92
National Partnership for Excellence and Accountability in Teaching, 80
National Science Education Standards, 24
New Standards Performance Standards, 35-37
New York City, 18, 49, 76-77, 84
Norm-referenced testing, 7, 8, 42, 43, 44, 48, 66-67
North Carolina, 16, 18, 19, 27, 30-32, 89, 99

O

Office of Bilingual Education and Language Minority Affairs, 61

P

Penalties, *see* Incentives and penalties
Performance standards, *vii*, 16-17, 23, 24, 33-41, 43, 91
    CRESST, 45
    defined, 4, 33-35
    education improvement systems, 3, 4, 5, 21
    English as a second language, 38-39
    fairness, 35, 47, 49
    federal role, 1, 10, 24, 42
    instructional methods, 33, 39-41
    mathematics, 15, 28, 33, 36-41
    multiple-purpose assessments, 46-47
    noneducational, 15-16
    norm-referenced testing, 7, 8, 42, 43, 44, 48, 66-67
    professional development, 82
    recommendations, 34-35
    reporting of results, 68-69
    state government role, 1, 9, 16, 33, 43, 45, 77-78
    Title I programs, 1, 10, 42
    validity, 45
    yearly progress requirements, 85-90
    see also Content standards

Pew Charitable Foundation, *vi*
Philadelphia, Pennsylvania, 19, 65-66, 77
Political factors, *v*, 11, 25
Portfolios, 4, 49, 52, 53, 54, 55, 81, 82, 83
Poverty, 10, 23-24, 47, 66, 71, 72, 73, 75, 78, 88
Privacy, 73
Professional development, 3, 20, 24, 26, 49, 79-84, 95
    curriculum, 79, 81
    school districts, 80, 81-82, 84
    state government role, 80, 81, 83
Promotion and retention in grade, 93-94

R

Reporting requirements, 48, 64, 66-70
    administrators, 69
    disaggregating data, 71-73, 78
    education improvement systems, 21
    federal role, 45, 55, 68, 70, 99
    performance standards, 68-69
    privacy, 73
    state government role, 68-70, 71, 72, 73
    teachers, 69, 70
Retention in grade, *see* Promotion and retention in grade
Rewards and sanctions, *see* Incentives and penalties

S

Sampling, 4, 88-89
San Antonio, Texas, 19
Sanctions and rewards, *see* Incentives and penalties
School district assessment, 4, 19, 21, 49-50
    accountability, 91, 96, 97, 100
    content standards, 26, 29
    early childhood education, 53, 57
    English-language learners, 62, 63, 64, 65-66
    individual student assessment, 55-56, 58-59
    instructional methods, 76-79
    reporting of results, 68-69, 71, 72
    professional development, 80, 81-82, 84
    students with disabilities, 55-56, 58-59
    validity issues, 45
    yearly progress requirements, 86, 89
    see also specific districts
School-level assessment, 4, 15, 17, 19, 23-24, 29, 73
    accountability, 6, 15, 17, 19, 65, 86, 87, 88, 89, 92-101 (passim)
    disaggregation of data, 71-72

instructional methods, 77, 78-79

internal accountability, 6, 19, 92-93, 98

professional development, 80

validity issues, 45-46

yearly progress requirements, 86-89 (passim)

Secondary education

science education standards, 24

students with disabilities, 60

Title I standards, 10

Title I students, number of, 1, 7

Second-language students, *see* English-language learners

Skills, *see* Performance standards

South Brunswick, New Jersey, 54

Special populations, 10, 14, 17

early childhood education, 51, 52

poor students, 10, 23-24, 47, 66, 71, 72, 73, 75, 78, 88

see also English-language learners; Students with disabilities

Spencer Foundation, *vi*

Standards, *v*

alignment, *iv, vii, x*, 2, 15, 17, 20, 26, 43-45, 75

assessment strategies, general, 1, 9-10, 16-17, 18, 42-50

education improvement systems, 3-6, 20, 21

English-language learners, 61-62

international perspectives, 16, 75

reform, standards-based, general, *v*, 2-3, 8-9, 11, 15-20, 23-24, 43, 74

reform, standards-based model, 16-18

reporting requirements, 21, 66-70

yearly progress requirements, 85-90

see also Accountability; Content standards; Performance standards

Standards for Educational and Psychological Testing, 46-47

Stanford Achievement Test, 65

State government, 1, 2, 9, 12

accountability efforts, 86-87, 88, 89-90, 91, 93, 95, 96-97, 99-101

alignment, tests and standards, 43-45

content standards, 1, 10, 24, 25, 26, 27-32, 43

early childhood education, 50-55

education improvement systems, 3, 5, 12, 21

English-language learners, 61, 62, 63, 64-65

instructional methods, 75-78

performance standards, 1, 9, 16, 33, 43, 45, 77-78

professional development, 80, 81, 83

reporting of results, 68-70, 71, 72, 73

standards-based reform, other, *v, vi, vii*, 8, 9, 10, 16, 18

student accountability, 94

students with disabilities, 55-56, 57, 58-60

yearly progress requirements, 86-87, 88, 89-90

see also specific states

Student assessment, individual, 4, 5, 8, 16, 21, 23-73, 77-78

accountability, 93-94

individualized education program, 55, 57

portfolios, 4, 49, 52, 53, 54, 55, 81, 82, 83

promotion and retention in grade, 93-94

sampling *vs*, 4

school districts, 55-56, 58-59

see also Content standards; English-language learners; Performance standards; Special populations; Students with disabilities

Students with disabilities, 5, 10, 21, 51, 55-60

accountability, 56

assessment strategies, 10, 21, 51, 55-60

federal role, 55, 56, 57, 58

individualized education programs, 55, 57, 59, 60

Individuals with Disabilities Education Act, 55, 56, 57

state government role, 55-56, 57, 58-60

validity issues, 56-59 (passim)

T

Teachers, 19-20, 74, 75-76

accountability, 6, 18, 19, 22, 52, 86, 92, 97, 98

assessments, 4, 5-6, 19-20, 47-48, 49-50, 53, 54-55

early childhood education, 52, 53

professional development, 3, 20, 24, 26, 49, 79-84, 95

reporting of results, 69, 70

yearly progress requirements, 86

Teachers of English to Students of Other Languages, 35, 61

Teaching, 2, 11, 20

content standards, 26

performance standards, 39-41

test-taking skills, 8, 42

see also Instructional methods

Texas, 16, 18, 19, 47, 65, 73, 99-101

Texas Assessment of Academic Skills, 65, 73, 99-101

Title I, *see* Federal government

U

University of Michigan, 54-55

V

Validity, 9, 21, 45-46, 48-49, 61, 63, 64, 67, 86,
        89
    content standards, 25-26
    early childhood testing, 52, 54
    English-language learners, 61, 63, 64
    performance standards, 45
    school/school-district assessment, 45-46
    students with disabilities, 56-59 (passim)
    see also Fairness
Vermont, 81, 83
Virginia, 25

W

Work Sampling System, 54-55
W.T. Grant Foundation, *vi*

Y

Yearly progress requirements, 85-90, 91